Octavivs Morgan

Some Account of the Ancient Monuments in the Priory Church, Abergavenny

Octavivs Morgan

Some Account of the Ancient Monuments in the Priory Church, Abergavenny

ISBN/EAN: 9783337003104

Printed in Europe, USA, Canada, Australia, Japan

Cover: Foto ©Lupo / pixelio.de

More available books at **www.hansebooks.com**

SOME ACCOUNT

OF THE

ANCIENT MONUMENTS

IN THE

PRIORY CHURCH,

ABERGAVENNY.

BY

OCTAVIUS MORGAN, Esq., M.P., F.R.S., F.S.A.,

President of the Monmouthshire and Caerleon Antiquarian Association.

1872.

PREFACE.

I have to offer very many apologies to the members of the Monmouthshire Antiquarian Association for the very great delay which has occurred in the production of the present book, which I regret to say has been so very long due. But I can assure them that it has not arisen from any wilful neglect, carelessness, or idleness on my part; and I must trust to their kind indulgence for forgiveness; for I fear that great disappointment has been the result of the delay. The work I found was one which I could not take up and write off hand; and had I known, when I promised to write an account of the Ancient Monuments, the length to which it would extend, and the number and variety of the subjects, the consideration of which would be necessary for a due explanation of these interesting remains, and the large amount of information on minute points which would be required, I should hardly have ventured to undertake the task; for I should have known well, that the completion of the work would have occupied a longer time than I should have wished, or indeed, properly speaking, should have had at my command; and that consequent delay in bringing out the book would occur, which must result in the disappointment which I fear has already been felt. I have, however, endeavoured fully to describe, explain, and illustrate these interesting remains, although I am well aware that the work has been but imperfectly done; and for the imperfections and shortcomings I must throw myself on the kind indulgence of our members.

O.M.

TABLE OF CONTENTS.

	PAGE
INTRODUCTION	1
BARONY OF ABERGAVENNY	3
ARMOUR OF XIII., XIV., AND XV. CENTURIES	8
CHURCHYARD'S POEM	15
THE MONUMENTS AND CHURCH	19
I.—GEORGE DE CANTELUPE ... *Wood.*	21
EFFIGIES AND FUNERALS	23
II.—SIR WILLIAM HASTINGS? ... *Stone.*	31
III.—LAWRENCE DE HASTINGS ... *Stone.*	36
IV.—SIR WILLIAM AP THOMAS ... *Alabaster.*	41
V.—SIR RICHARD HERBERT, OF COLDBROOK ... *Alabaster.*	56
VI.—SIR RICHARD HERBERT, OF EWYAS ... *Alabaster.*	63
VII.—EVA DE BRAOSE? ... *Stone.*	70
VIII.—EVA DE CANTELUPE ... *Stone.*	72
IX.—JUDGE ANDREW POWELL ... *Stone.*	75
X.—DR. DAVID LEWIS ... *Stone.*	79
XI.—FIGURE OF JESSE ... *Wood.*	85

PHOTOGRAPHIC ILLUSTRATIONS.

I.—GEORGE DE CANTELUPE.
II.—SIR WILLIAM HASTINGS?
III.—LAWRENCE DE HASTINGS.
IV.—SIR WILLIAM AP THOMAS.
V.— DITTO   DITTO.
VI.—SIR RICHARD HERBERT, OF COLDBROOK.
VII.— DITTO   DITTO.
VIII.—SIR RICHARD HERBERT, OF EWYAS.
IX.—EVA DE BRAOSE?
X.—EVA DE CANTELUPE.
XI.—JUDGE ANDREW POWELL.
XII.—DR. DAVID LEWIS.
XIII.—FIGURE OF JESSE.

SOME ACCOUNT

OF THE

MONUMENTS IN THE PRIORY CHURCH,

AT ABERGAVENNY.

The Monuments in the Priory Church, at Abergavenny, have long been objects of interest, especially to those who have carefully examined and studied them. They have not, however, received that attention which they deserve, nor have they in times past experienced that care which they have merited. It is, indeed, sad to see the wanton injuries and disfigurements to which these beautiful works of art have been subjected at some period in days gone by; but of late years more care has been taken of them, and further mischief prevented; and it is to be hoped, now that attention has been directed to them, what remains may be carefully preserved from further mutilation, as well as from injudicious restoration. They all seem to have been much injured at some particular period, and to have been subsequently rudely and inartistically repaired; and many of the parts seem to have been misplaced, if they did not belong to some other structures.

These Monuments are very instructive on three grounds.—First: they form a remarkably good and most instructive series of monumental effigies from the XIII to the XVII century, shewing the various forms and characters of such structures, and displaying in an admirable manner the various changes which successively took place in the arms and armour of the knightly warriors; exhibiting a valuable and consecutive series of illustrations, not only of armour, but also of costume, as well of ladies as of knights, during a period of four centuries. The second ground of interest is that this series of Monuments affords beautiful examples of the various substances which have been used for the construction of monumental effigies, wood, stone, alabaster, and formerly of brass or bronze; and the examples are all of remarkably good type and character, and I think it will be difficult to find a Church which can exhibit so complete and regular a series, for there are not only the effigies and tombs of men, but we have those also of ladies. Thirdly and lastly; we have the historical interest attached to them, as being the Monuments of distinguished personages connected not only with the special locality, but also with the general history of the country, and I hope to be able to identify these early effigies, respecting which there are now doubts.

The Church of Abergavenny, however, is not an ordinary Parish Church, having been originally the Church and Chapel of the Priory, and the Monks settled there. This Priory was a Monastery of Benedictine or Black Monks, founded in the reign of Henry I. (1100—1135), by Hameline de Balun or Baladun, the first Norman Lord of Abergavenny, and was therefore intimately connected with the Lordship, and was at a subsequent period further endowed by, and received gifts from several of his successors.

The town of Abergavenny was the Capital of the Lordship, and was a walled town; and the ancient Parish Church of St. John stood within the walls; the Priory and its Church being outside the town by the East Gate. After the dissolution of the Monasteries, in 1543, Henry VIII founded the Grammar School, which he endowed with some of the possessions of the suppressed Priory, and granted the old Parish Church of St. John as the site for his new school, and at that time, in all probability, the Priory Church, instead of being pulled down as was frequently the case, was granted in lieu of it for the parish Church; and it is very likely that the North Aisle was added at that time.

At the dissolution, the establishment of the Priory consisted of a Prior and only four Monks; and according to Mr. Wakeman, in 1546, all the possessions of the Monastery, which amounted in value to £80 per annum, were granted to James Gunter, of Breconshire, and continued in his family till the beginning of the last century, when Mary, daughter and heiress of James Gunter, of the Priory, married George Milbourne, of Wonastow, and so conveyed the Priory Estates to him, and they, together with Wonastow, descended to their son Charles, who married Lady Martha Harley, daughter of the Earl of Oxford, and their only daughter and heiress Mary carried them to her husband, Thomas Swinnerton, Esq., of Butterton, in Staffordshire, whose daughter and co-heiress married Charles Kemeys Tynte, Esq.

It will be necessary to give a short account of the Barony of Abergavenny, and the various personages who held the Lordship, as reference will hereafter be made to many of them; and for this I am greatly indebted to the beautiful "History of the Neville Family," by Rowland Williams, Esq.; as also to the papers of the late Thomas Wakeman, Esq., the careful and accurate historian of our local Antiquarian Association, whose loss we all have so much reason to lament.

THE BARONY OF ABERGAVENNY.

The Honor or Lordship of Abergavenny is one of the most Ancient Baronies, and was probably granted very soon after the conquest, when divers Princely Baronies were formed with Royal or Palatine powers, for the purpose of guarding the country against the incursions of the Welsh. The Earldom of Chester was planted in the North Border of Wales and was erected into a county Palatine. In the south borders many Baronies and Lordships were also erected, stretching from Chester to the Severn, called Lordship's Marches, having Palatine jurisdiction, a court of Chancery, and writs and pleadings of their own, with powers of life and death; and into them the Kings's writs did not run. The Lordship of Abergavenny was one of the most important and powerful of these, and was at one time considered a Barony by tenure, which entitled the possessor of it to a writ of summons to Parliament; a detailed history of it would be out of place, and it will be sufficient to enumerate the list of Barons, with such few particulars as may be necessary to shew the descent.

I. The first Baron is usually believed to be Drogo or Dru de Baladun, or Balun, (supposed to be Boulogne), who came over with William the Conqueror. He was Lord of Abergavenny in the reign of Henry I; and the Lordship granted consisted of the country of Overwent, which he held in capite of the King, and was to defend it at his own cost and charges against the Welsh : he was succeeded by his son,

II. Hameline de Balun, who probably built a castle, and founded the Priory in the reign of Henry I.; having no issue, he bequeathed his estates to his nephew, Brian de" Insula," son of his youngest sister Lucy. He died before 1128, and is believed to have been buried in the Priory.

III. (1128). Bryan de Insula, *alias* De Wallingford, was in possession of the estates of his uncle in 1128. He had two sons, whom as they were afflicted with leprosy, he placed in the Priory of Abergavenny, and on their account made large grants and endowments to the institution. On account of the incapacity of his sons, he gave his Barony to his cousin Walter of Gloucester, and departed for the Holy Land, where he died. He was a strong supporter of the Empress Maud in her wars with King Stephen.

IV. Walter of Gloucester, son of Milo Fitz Walter, Earl of Hereford, and Emma, sister of Hameline de Balun, was High Constable of England ; having no issue, he granted his Barony to his younger brother Henry, and retiring from the world, became a Monk in the Priory of Llanthony, where he died and was buried.

V. Henry, of Hereford, 4th son of Milo Fitz Walter, Earl of Hereford, to which Earldom on the death of his brother Roger he succeeded, becoming at the same time Lord of Brecknock and the Forest of Dean; Sitsyllt ap Dyfnwall, Lord of Castle Arnold, succeeded in drawing him into his power and murdered him. He had no issue, and his Baronies and Estates passed to his sisters and their children. The regular descent was by this event interrupted for a short time, but was soon restored in the person of

VI. William de Braose, who was son of Philip de Braose and Bertha, second daughter of Milo Fitz Walter, and co-heiress of her brother Henry the last Baron. In 1172, the castle of Abergavenny was surprised and taken by Sitsyllt ap Dyfnwall, but was restored to de Braose in 1176, and subsequently in revenge de Braose invited Sitsyllt and his son and others to a festivity at the castle, and then treacherously massacred them, and proceeding to Castle Arnold murdered the wife and infant child, and took possession of the estates. He became suspected by King John, who banished him and seized his estates, and having escaped to France died in Paris 1213.

VII. Giles, Bishop of Hereford, eldest surviving son of William de Braose the elder, and uncle to the last Baron, ultimately obtained from the King the restitution of a large portion of the family estates, and died 1215, leaving his possessions to his brother Reginald.

VIII. Reginald de Braose, who in 1217 had a grant of safe conduct into the King's presence, had also a grant of a great part of his father and brother's lands. He married Griselda, daughter of William, Lord Bruere, and left issue William and John, and a daughter. He died 1222; and in the same year William de Cantelupe and John of Monmouth were ordered to seize his castles.

IX. William de Braose, his eldest son, (called junior, to distinguish him from his grandfather), succeeded him. He was true to the King, and being hostile to the Welsh, united his forces with those of Henry III against them. He was taken prisoner in the war by Llewellyn, Prince of North Wales, who refused ransom, and caused him to be hanged in 1230. He married Eva, daughter of William Marshall, Earl of Pembroke, but had no male issue, and left only four daughters, who were all under age at their father's death. Eva married William de Cantelupe, of whom hereafter. Eleonora was wife of Humphry de Bohun; Matilda married Roger Mortimer, of Wigmore; and Isabella married David Prince of Wales. Upon a partition of the estates between the sisters, Abergavenny fell to the share of Eva, who in 1238 was given in ward to William de Cantelupe, a powerful Baron of Aston Cantelupe, in the county of Warwick; and in 1248 she was married to William de Cantelupe the son of her guardian, who thereupon had livery of her estates.

X. William de Cantelupe, son and heir of William Lord Cantelupe, held the Lordship of Abergavenny in right of his wife Eva, daughter and co-heiress of William de Braose the last Lord, and was summoned to parliament by the King's writ under the style and title of Baron of

Burgavenny, by which name the Lordship continued to be called for a very long period. He died in 1256, and was succeeded in the Barony by his wife, by whom he left issue a son George, about three years of age, and two daughters, Milicent, who afterwards married Ivo de la Zouch, and Joan, who married Henry, Lord Hastings.

XI. (1256). Eva, widow of William de Cantelupe, the last Lord, succeeded her husband in the Lordship as Baroness in her own right, but she did not survive him above a year, and died in 1257, leaving her son George, a minor, only four years old.

XII. (1257). George, Lord Cantelupe, succeeded to the Barony on the death of his mother, but being only four years old, was on account of his minority in ward to the King, in whose hands were the castle and Lordship. He gave them into the custody of John Breton, Bishop of Hereford, but in 1265 they seem to have been in the hands of the rebellious Barons, as Simon de Montfort conveyed hither the King, then a prisoner, but soon removed him to Hereford. George married the daughter of Edmund Lacy, Earl of Lincoln, and had by her a son who died during his life time, and he himself died in 1273 at the age of twenty, being the last Lord of the line of Cantelupe, and leaving his estates and manors to be divided between his two sisters, Milicent and Joan; and upon the partition, to Joan the youngest, who had married Henry, Lord Hastings, was awarded the Lordship of Abergavenny, and the manors and estates in Wales. Henry, Lord Hastings, the husband of Joan, died in 1268, leaving a son John de Hastings, a minor, who therefore succeeded to the Barony of Burgavenny as heir, on the death of George the last Baron.

XIII. (1273). John de Hastings, being a minor, hardly more than a year old, was confided by the King to the care of William de Valence, Earl of Pembroke, who in 1283 had also charge of the castle. Upon attaining his majority he did homage and had livery of his lands, and married first Isabella daughter of his guardian William de Valence, (who afterwards became co-heiress to her brother Aymer de Valence), and in 1295 was summoned to Parliament as Lord Hastings, though he was unquestionably Baron of Burgavenny. He particularly distinguished himself in the wars in France and Scotland, and died in 1313, seized of the Lordship of Abergavenny which he held of the King in capite, and if war should happen between the King and the Prince of Wales, he was bound to keep the country of Overwent at his own charge for his own benefit and for the King's use. By his first wife he had a son John, who succeeded him, and a daughter Elizabeth, who married Lord Grey de Ruthyn. He married secondly, Isabel, daughter of Hugh Despenser, Earl of Winchester, and had other issue.

XIV. (1313). John de Hastings, son of the preceding, and called junior to distinguish him from his father whom he succeeded, being twenty-six years of age. In 1317 he was charged to raise 200 foot soldiers from his estates in Gwent for the Scotch Wars, when he served under his maternal uncle, Aymer de Valence, Earl of Pembroke. In 1322 he was ordered to raise 400 men in Gwent, by a second writ, and 300 men out of Abergavenny and Gwent for the King's service. He married Juliana, daughter and heiress of Thomas de Leybourne, and died 1325, seized of the castle and Lordship; leaving a son and heir Lawrence, a minor. His widow within a year married Thomas Le Blound, and thirdly, William de Clinton, Earl of Huntingdon.

XV. (1325). Lawrence de Hastings succeeded his father when very young, and being a minor, both he and his estates were in ward to the King, who in 1337 committed him to the custody of William de Clinton, Earl of Huntingdon, who had married his mother, with a yearly allowance of 200 marks, equal to £133 : 6 : 8 out of the exchequer. The castle and estates were given into the custody of various parties in succession. He came of age in 1339, and on the 13th of October was created Earl of Pembroke on account of his descent from Isabella, the eldest sister and co-heiress of Aylmer de Valence, and the same year he accompanied the King in his expedition to Flanders, and in the year following he was in the naval battle of Sluys, when the French fleet was defeated. In 1344 he attended the King into Britany with six men at arms, two bannerets, twelve knights, forty-five esquires, and one hundred archers on horseback. The names of this company are not recorded, but there can be no doubt that many of his Gwentian retainers and tenants were among them. He remained in Britany till the following year, when he served in Gascony under Henry, Duke of Lancaster in the 18th, 19th, 20th and 21st of Edward III, and in 1348 he died seized of the Lordship and Castle of Abergavenny, leaving by his wife Agnes, daughter of Roger Mortimer, Earl of March, John his son and heir, then only one year old, and was buried at the Priory at Abergavenny. His widow married John de Hackelut, and at her death in 1368, bequeathed to the Priory "of Burgavenny, where my Lord lieth buried, a suit of rich vestments of green cloth of gold." He had a half-brother, who was illegitimate and was called Sir William de Hastings, to whom he was much attached, and gave him several manors and estates out of his Lordship of Abergavenny, which, however, reverted to the superior Lord, Sir William dying without issue, 23rd March, 1349.

XVI. (1369). John de Hastings Lord of Abergavenny and Earl of Pembroke, the third of that name, being only one year old at his father's death, came of age in 1369, the year after his mother's death. He married Anna, only daughter and heiress of Sir Walter Manney, and with her had the Lordship of Chepstow and other extensive possessions. For this marriage he was obliged to obtain a special dispensation from the Pope, inasmuch as he had formerly married Margaret, daughter of King Edward III, she being allied to Margaret in the third and fourth degrees of consanguinity; for this he gave 1000 florins of gold for the repair of the church and monastery at Urbino. This John de Hastings was an eminent commander in the wars in France under the Black Prince; and in 1372 for his valour was created a Knight of the Garter, and made the King's Lieutenant of Aquitaine, whither he was sent with a reinforcement of troops and 2000 marks in money to carry on the war against the French and Spaniards. In that expedition he was unfortunate, for the enemy's fleet lay off Rochelle, and although he maintained, the contest for two whole days against a greatly superior force, he and many others were taken prisoners, and all his ships burnt sunk, or taken. He remained a prisoner till 1373, when he was ransomed, but died at Calais on his way home on the 16th April, (it was reported that he had been poisoned by the Spaniards,) being seized of the Lordships of Abergavenny, Chepstow, and many others; and leaving John his son, only two years and a half old. He was buried at the church of the Friars Preachers, at Hereford, but the body was afterwards for the sum of £100 (equal to £1500 of modern money,) translated to the Grey Friars in London. His widow Ann held the Castle and Lordship in dower, and died seized thereof in 1381, John her son being then only eleven years old.

XVII. John de Hastings, son and heir of the last Lord of Abergavenny and Earl of Pembroke, being only three years old at his father's death, was a ward of the Crown, and his castles and estates were in the King's hands. At the coronation of Richard II, 1381, being then according to Dugdale, eleven years old, he claimed to carry the gold spurs, and having proved his right, it was adjudged that by reason of his minority, he should be allowed to perform the service by deputy. The office was served for him by Edmund Mortimer, Earl of March, whose daughter Phillippa he seems to have married, although so young. He lived but to attain the age of seventeen; for in the year 1389 the King was keeping his Christmas at Woodstock, and on the 13th December, at the tournament held that day, he ventured to tilt with Sir John St. John, and by an unfortunate slip of Sir John's lance, it entered his body and produced instant death. He was buried in the Church of the Grey Friars in London, where according to Stowe there was a splendid monument erected over him, which remained till after the dissolution of the religious houses under Henry VIII, when it was destroyed.

As he had no issue, he was the last Lord of Abergavenny of the line of Hastings, and his title of Earl of Pembroke ceased at his death. The Baronies however which were vested in him, devolved by law upon Reginald Lord Grey de Ruthyn as descended lineally from Elizabeth sister John de Hastings, the father of Lawrence, who was the first Earl of Pembroke. The Earl of March claimed the dower of his widowed daughter, and after some disputes the third part of the Castle and Lordship was assigned to her, and the subsequent descent of the Lordship and estates was a fruitful source of long disputes and litigation. With that descent we have nothing to do, as it has no relation to the Monuments which we have to consider.

SOME REMARKS

ON THE

ANCIENT ARMOUR OF THE XIII, XIV, & XV CENTURIES.

As in the examination of these Monuments we shall be much guided by the Armour displayed upon them, as being most probably an exact representation of that which was actually worn by the persons whom they were intended to commemorate, or if not their very Armour, certainly that which was worn at the period of their deaths, I think it may be desirable to give a brief description of the defensive Armour worn by Knights during the XIII, XIV, and XV centuries, with such explanations as will make the subject generally intelligible, which a simply strict adherence to technical terms might not be. Our chief authorities on this subject are supplied by monuments, knightly effigies of known date, manuscript illuminations, seals, chasings in metal, carvings in ivory, and the writers of chronicles and metrical romances.

The armour of a Man-at-Arms during the XIII century, and till nearly the middle of the XIV century, consisted of the following particulars : a loose garment stuffed with cotton or wool, and quilted, covering the body, called a gambeson, from the French word gamboisé ; and it may be here remarked that most of the names of the various parts of armour are taken from the Norman or French. Over this was worn a coat of mail, formed of double rings or mascles of iron interwoven like the meshes of a net, called a hauberk ; this hauberk was a complete covering of mail from head to foot ; it consisted of a hood joined to a jacket with sleeves, also breeches, stockings, and shoes of double chain mail all in one piece ; to which were added gloves or gauntlets of the same. These gauntlets had an opening in the palm through which the hand could be passed when it was required to put them off. In the second half of the XIII century the fingers began to be divided, probably from improved skill in the manufacture. In the hood, which was continuous from the coat of mail of the body, and called the coif, there was an aperture for the face, and in the early part of the century the top of the head was frequently formed nearly flat, but the round topped coif is found throughout the century. It was frequently surrounded by a fillet or band, sometimes plain, sometimes ornamented. There was also another kind of chain mail introduced at a later period, having the appearance of rows or bands of rings laid one over another. I believe no instance exists, and its construction is not very well understood. The coif was drawn over the head by means of an opening in the side, which was fastened up with a strap or lace. The upper part above the face was towards the end of the century occasionally replaced or covered by a skull cap or cervelliére of iron plate, and which was probably the origin of the bascinet. Sometimes the sleeves of the hauberk terminated at the wrist, the gloves or gauntlets being separate. To the elbows of the hauberk were sometimes affixed towards the close of the century plates of metal called coudiéres ; the covering of the legs were called chausses, and in the early part of the century covered the whole leg, but afterwards poleyns or knee pieces of plate were occasionally added, and towards the close of the century they were accompanied with a chausson of leather or quilted work on the thighs, probably to obviate the inconvenience of long chausses of chain mail in riding. The armour of chain mail was cleaned by rolling it in a barrel, probably with sand.

The head was further defended by a helmet of various forms, worn over the hood of chain mail in battle. These helms were frequently of cylindrical form, with narrow slits to admit air and enable the wearer to see. Over the hauberk was worn a loose surcoat, a loose garment without sleeves, reaching below the knees, and which, in the case of persons of considerable distinction, were of rich materials, and charged with their armorial bearings ; hence the term coat of arms. The hauberk and surcoat which was open in front part of the way to the waist, were girt round the body with a leather strap or belt, called the balteus, and by the French baudrier, we are told from being made of tanned leather ; whence our term baldrick. To this belt was attached the sword, which was straight, of large size, and had a cross hilt. A leather thong called the guige passed round the neck, from which the shield was suspended. The earliest shields were of the long heater form, and they became shorter as the century advanced towards the end, when they were nearly triangular.

At first the hauberk, hood, and sleeves were all of one piece ; but in process of time, when the chapel de fer and afterwards the bascinet were introduced as a covering for the head, the hood was separated from the hauberk, and fastened by a lace to the bascinet, and covering the throat, fell over the neck upon the shoulders like a tippet, and was called the camail. This at a much later period was formed of plate and was called the gorget or throat piece, and was the last piece of plate armour used, having been continued, though in a very diminished size, and as an ornament only, till within the last forty years. When, in process of time, the hood and sleeves were separated from the hauberk, it was called a haubergeon, which is therefore a hauberk without hood or sleeves. The haketon was a garment stuffed or wadded, worn above the shirt, and under the haubergeon, as the gambeson was under the hauberk, and was probably of lighter materials. The heels of the knights were equipped with spurs, which were generally the goad or prick spur of short length, the rowel being only found in one or two instances at the end of the century.

The XIV century was essentially a period of transition in all military matters of attack and defence, the invention and use of gunpowder operating to produce great changes. The body armour offers many diversities of form, but towards the end of the century there is more uniformity. The materials employed were iron, steel, brass, leather, whalebone, and the stuffs used for quilted defences. The iron was worn in the form of chain mail, scale work, splinted or studded armour and plate: splinted armour was of two kinds, either having the metal strips or splints in view, or having the splints covered with leather or a textile material of quilted pourpointerie, with the studs of the rivets which fasten them together appearing on the surface like small roundels, and being frequently gilt. Pourpoint or pourpointerie, from the latin *per punctum*, indicates its construction, being composed of several thicknesses of material sewed through and faced with silk or velvet, on which armorial bearings were embroidered, and thus the garment was frequently called pourpoint; its manufacture was a special trade in Paris, which was under particular regulations to prevent the making and selling fraudulent stuffs. Brass was only used for ornamental purposes; but the jacked leather, called cuir bouilli, which consisted of hides hardened and rendered waterproof by being boiled, probably in oil, and pressed into shape in moulds was often substituted for metal in the defences of the body, legs, and arms; and, indeed, bascinets of cuir bouilli have been mentioned; the material being smooth and rigid, it is impossible to distinguish articles made of it from those of metal in sculpture and pictures. Quilted or pourpoint garments occur throughout the period, sometimes as the undercoat of a steel defence, sometimes as the principal body armour, and sometimes as the armorial surcoat. Defences of iron and steel are often mentioned for body, arms, and legs; and plate armour, whether of metal or other rigid substance came gradually into use as the century advanced, till at its close the old fabric of chain mail is only seen at the bottom of the skirt, and at the neck. Isolated examples may be found of the plate gorget and plate tassets at the hips, but it is not till the XV century, by the general adoption of these pieces, the knight became encased in plate armour.

The body defence of plate is variously termed "plates of steel," "a breast plate," and a pair of plates. These were at first worn under the quilted garment, but were afterwards worn externally, and at length, supplanting the quilted garment, became a full suit of body armour. A great change was now made in the surcoat, which had been a long loose garment open to a certain extent up the front for the convenience of riding; but when the horsemen adopted the practice of dismounting at times, and fighting on foot, this long garment was found inconvenient, and the front part was cut away. This uneven surcoat was still inconvenient, and certainly unsightly, and the shears being applied behind, it was shortened all round. The full skirt, a necessity of the long dress, had now neither use nor meaning; it was therefore abandoned, and the garment became the short close-fitting surcoat, familiar to us in the monuments of the middle and latter part of the century, and to this the name of jupon was frequently given. The arm defences are various; those of plate alone are seen as early as 1325, but they are not general till the middle or latter half of the century. The earliest were roundels, or discs, affixed to the sleeve of mail to protect the joints of the shoulder and arm: the jointed epaulettes first appear in the second quarter of the century, and form a shoulder cap. The elbow pieces, coudières, were either disc-formed, cup-shaped, or articulated; and they are combined, with much variety, with the other parts of the dress, until towards the end of the century the whole arm was encased in plate. The gauntlets exhibit a similar progress with the rest of the armour, beginning with chain mail, and offering as they advance various examples of scale work, stud work, and other fabrics. About the middle of the century arose the use of plate gauntlets, the fingers being articulated, the remainder of a broad piece or pieces, and in some there is a show of a leather cuff.

The leg harness of the knights made a similar steady progress towards complete equipment in plate. The old fabrics of chain mail, scale work, pourpointerie, splint, and stud work are of frequent appearance. In the first quarter these are all found; by the end of the second quarter the full arming of plate is attained, and in the second half it became general. Chain mail chausses of the XIII century are of frequent occurrence in the early part. This leg armour consisted of three parts—the chaussons with the genouilleres attached, the greaves or leg armour, and the solleret or armed shoe. The knee piece formed part of the chausson, and was strapped on the leg; the chaussons were frequently of leather, or quilted splint work, having the studs or rivets outside; the greaves were either of chain mail, cuir bouilli, or some splint work with the splints outside, or all plate, and were at times highly ornamented. Some may have been of cuir bouilli, to which a highly ornamental surface might be given by pressure in a mould: these leg defences now ended in an entire casing of plate. The armour for the feet passed through similar phases, being at first of chain or banded mail, but when greaves were introduced as the covering of the shin, the covering of the feet, then called sollerets, was composed either of scale work, or of a series of articulated joints from the instep to the toe; the back of the leg, heel, and sole remaining of chain mail. When the back of the leg was protected by plate, the heel and whole foot were also defended in a similar way. The spur characteristic of the XIV century is of the rowel kind, with the arms curving under the ankle, the neck short and straight; the goad or prick spur is, however, not uncommon.

The head defences of this century consisted of the bascinet with the camail, and the helm or heaume. The bascinet was a conical pointed cap of iron, of curvilinear form, terminating in a rounded point; in front it was cut away in a square form for the face, and to it was fastened by a lace the hood or tippet of chain mail, called the camail. The border of the bascinet was frequently enriched with ornamental work. Sometimes the bascinet had a visor attached to it, which could be raised or lowered, or removed at pleasure; this visor was pierced with holes, to enable the wearer to see and breathe. With this visor the warrior might go into battle without his helm, which was very large and heavy, and only worn in battle, or at a tournament. The helms were of various forms; the lower part being generally somewhat in form of a cylinder, and having a conical top, on which was fixed the crest with its mantling: there were small apertures made for the admission of breathing air, and to enable the knight to see; but they were very small.

The shields of this century offer considerable diversity of form. The most usual are the triangular or heater shaped, the heart shaped, the circular or round buckler, or the curved or notched shield, according to the time of the century. The materials were leather, cuir bouilli, and wood, sometimes covered with iron or steel. They occasionally displayed armorial bearings, and were suspended at the neck by the guige, and had also enarmes or straps by which they were attached to the arm. The knightly sword was broad, straight, and two edged, acutely pointed with a simple cross piece for its guard, and the pommel shewed a variety of forms. The scabbard was usually of leather, either embellished with stamped ornaments or mounted in gilt metal, the patterns of which were those employed in the architectural enrichments of the day. The sword belt underwent great changes, from being the mere strap for suspension of the weapon, it gradually increased in richness till it became the most brilliant and costly portion of the knight's equipment: the precious metals, enamels, and even jewels were used in its construction, and the skill of the goldsmith was taxed to furnish the most elaborate designs. The old method of arrangement is still found in the early monuments; but when the tight surcoat came into fashion, the military belt also became tight, and it was bound round the hips in a manner which seems to be most inconvenient. This enriched belt was sometimes prolonged; and the portion hanging from beyond the clasp or buckle was called the pendant; these pendants were much embellished and terminated in a highly enriched ornament. The dagger does not commonly appear on knightly monuments till the second quarter of the century, but after that it is very frequent; it was suspended by a chain from the belt on the right side, and varied much in size and form.

By the XV century, defences of plate armour had been generally adopted, and the differences of suits of armour are principally differences of form; and as numerous suits and examples of real armour and weapons of this age are to be found in many collections, there is no longer the same uncertainty as to their forms or construction. Chain or banded mail still however continued to be used; but the plates for the defences of the breast and back had become the outer defences of the body, and the jupon or short surcoat is rarely found beyond the first quarter of the century. The breast and back plates terminated at the waist, and the defences below the waist were formed of overlapping hoops of iron or steel called tassets, and the skirt of mail terminating in an escaloped edge appears beneath them. The gorget of mail was partly covered by the plate gorget, and ultimately superseded by it; the visored bascinet gives place to the salade with the mentoniere or chin plate; this was a round topped skull cap, with a chin piece attached to it, which was fixed, whilst the upper part followed the movement of the head. The shoulder pieces of many articulated strips of metal are superseded by a pauldron of broad plates, and these plates overlapping the defaut de la cuirasse at the joint of the arm, displace the gussets of steel or roundell plates in front of each arm. As the century advances the tassets, instead of terminating in a wide hoop, have tile pieces or tuiles attached to them by hinges or straps, at first very small, but gradually increasing in length, and the number of the tasset hoops decreasing, till at the end of the century we find them of great size covering the thighs like large flaps, whilst the number of the tasset hoops is reduced from seven to three. The skirt of chain mail still shews below them, and frequently terminates in a point in the centre. The sollerets of natural form and ingenious construction give way to the long toed cracowe, terminating in a long sharp point, which was absurd in appearance and most inconvenient in use; and the spurs, at first of moderate dimensions, were laid aside for others of preposterous length of neck, and remarkable for the great size of the rowel. As the century advances the excess of fashion in armour became ludicrous from the great size of the pauldrons, and fantastic and inconvenient forms of the elbow plates. The armour of the thighs and legs is of plate throughout the century, without anything remarkable beyond some large and inconvenient plates attached to the genouilleres. The sword and dagger continued much as before, but with the jupon the large and costly belt on the hips was dispensed with, and the sword was supported by a strap passing across the body in a slanting direction, not remarkable for its decoration. With this I may close the brief and imperfect account I have endeavoured to give of the armour worn at the time when the heroes of our monuments flourished; but I think it will be found sufficient to guide us in the consideration of the matters which may come under our review.

CHURCHYARD'S POEM.

We have some early notices of these Monuments. The first is a description of Abergavenny, the Castle, Church, and Monuments in a poem instituted "The Worthiness of Wales," written near the end of the XVI century by Thomas Churchyard. He lived in the time of Queen Elizabeth, and seems to have made a tour in Wales in 1586; that is between the time of the death of Dr. David Lewis in 1585, and the publication of his poem in 1587. This tour he has described in a poem which he has called "The Worthiness of Wales," and dedicated it to Her Most Excellent Majesty Queen Elizabeth; and as this poem is but little known, and gives much information respecting the church and the monuments, I have thought it desirable to give at length so much of it as relates to the subject. He seems to have greatly admired the monuments, and has given a long description of them as accurately as his verses would permit, and it is clear that they were then in perfect condition, and the church must have presented a very different appearance when the windows displayed in stained glass the escutcheons of the families of the different Lords, and coats of arms were emblazoned on the different monuments. The poem was first published in 1587, and subsequently reprinted in 1776. It is from the latter edition that I have transcribed the poem together with the marginal notes, which in some places amplify, supplement, and explain the text.

In the "Diary of the Marchings of the Royal Army" in 1645, kept by Richard Symonds, who accompanied King Charles I in his visit to Monmouthshire in that year, we have in some respects a more detailed account of the monuments and stained glass windows, with their armorial bearings, in the Priory Church at Abergavenny. Symonds seems to have kept an exact account of everything monumental, genealogical, and armorial in every church and mansion in the various parts of the country through which he passed. These descriptions will be noticed when we come to the respective monuments. Richard Symond's diary was printed by the Camden Society in 1859.

These Monuments are also mentioned by Gough in his edition of Camden, in the additions which he made to the original text, from a manuscript in his possession, dated July 8, 1646. This must have been prior to the destruction, as they were all standing undisturbed at that date; and since that time we have no record of them, and it neither seems to be known at what precise time they were destroyed, nor when they were repaired.

CHURCHYARD'S POEM.

Extract of so much of the Poem of Thomas Churchyard, called "The worthiness of Wales," as relates to the Monuments in the Priory Church at Abergavenny.

In this Church a most famous worke in maner of a genealogie of Kings, called the roote of Jesse, which worke is defaced and pulled downe in peeces.	Though castle here through trackt of tyme is worne A church remaines that worthie is of note: Where worthie men that hath bene nobly borne Were layd in tombe, which els had been forgot, And buried cleane in grave past mynd of man As thousands are, forgot since world began: Whose race was great, and who for want of tome In dust doth dwell, unknowne till day of dome.
No. II. On the right hand in a faire chappell.	In church there lyes a noble knight, Enclosde in wall right well: Cross legged as it seems to sight (Or as record doth tell).
Both the window and other parts about him shew that he was a stranger.	He was of high and princely blood, His armes doth shew the same, For thereby may be understood, He was a man of fame. His shield of blacke he bears on brest, A white crowe plaine thereon: A ragged sleeve in top and crest, All wrought in goodly stone, And under feete a greyhound lyes,
Blewe is the labell whereon are nyne flower-de-luces.	Three golden lyons gay, Nine flower-de-luces there likewise His arms doth full display.
No. III. On the left hand a Lord of Aborgany.	A Lord that once enjoyde that seate Lyes there in sumptuous sort; They say as loe his race was great, So aunctent men report. His force was much, for he by strength With Bull did struggle so, He broke cleane off his hornes at length, And therewith let him go. This Lord a bull hath under feete, And as it may be thought A dragon under head doth lye, In stone full finely wrought. The worke and tombe so aunctent is (And of the earliest guyse), My first bare view, full well may mis, To shewe how well he lyes.
No. IV. Sir William Thomas, Knight. *alias* Harbert.	A tombe indeede of charge and showe Amid the chappell stands: Where William Thomas, knight ye knowe Lyes long, with stretched hands; A Harbert was he cal'd of right, Who from great kindred cam,
Sir David Gam father to this Knight's wife.	And married to a worthy wight Daughter to Davie Gam, (A knight likewise of right and name),

This Knight was slain at Edgincourt field.

His tombe is of hard and good alabaster.

Sir William Thomas was father to the next that followes, called Sir Richard Harbert, of Colbroke, Knight.

No. V.

In the chronicle this is rehearsed.

On the left hand of the chappell they lye.

She was daughter to Thomas ap Griffith, father to Sir Rice ap Thomas, knight.

This Harbert and his feere
Lyes there like one that purchast fame
As plainely doth appeere.
His tombe is rich and rare to viewe
Well wrought of great devicc
Though it be old, tombes made but new
Are of no greater price.
His armes three ramping lyons white
Behind his head in shield :
A crowned lyon black is hers
Set out in most rich field :
Behind her head is likewise there,
Loe what our elders did
To make those famous every where
Whose vertues are not hid.

In tombe as trim as that before
Sir Richard Harbert lyes :
He was at Banbrie field of yore
And through the battaile twise
He passed with pollax in his hands,
A manly act indeede
To preace among so many bands,
As you of him may rede.
This valiant knight at Colbroke dwelt,
Nere Aborgaynie towne,
Who when his fatall destnie felt
And fortune flong him downe.
Among his enemies lost his head,
A rufull tale to tell :
Yet buryed was as I have said
In sumptuous tombe full well,
His wife, Dame Margret, by his side
Lyes there likewise for troth ;
There armes as yet may be tryed
(In honor of them both),
Stands at their heads three lyons white,
He gives as well he might
Three ravens blacke in shield she gives,
As daughter to a knight ;
A sheafe of arrowes under head
He hath as due to him ;
Thus there these worthie couple lye
In tombe full fine and trim.

No. VI.
On the right hand of the chappell.

Now in another passing tombe
Of beautie and of charge,
There lyes a squire (that Harbert hight)
With cost set out at large.
Two daughters and sixe sonnes also
Are there set nobly forth ;
With other workes that makes the showe
And monument more worth.
Himselfe his wife, and children toe
Lyes shrouded in that seate.

The old Earle of Pembroke, one of the Privy Counsell.

Now somewhat for that squire I do,
Because his race was great.
He was the father of that earle,
That dyed Lord Steward late,
A man of might, of spreet most rare,
And borne to happie fate.
His father layed so richly here,
So long agoe withall
Shewes to the lookers on full cleere,
(When this to mynd they call)
This squire was of an auncient race,
And borne of noble blood,
Sith that he dyed in such a cace,
And left such wordly good,
To make a tombe so rich and brave :
Nay further now to say,
The three white lyons that he gave
In armes doth rare bewray :
And makes them blush and hold downe browe,
That babble out of square,
Rest there and to my matter now ;
Upon this tombe there are
Three lyons and three white bore's heads,
The first three are his owne.
The white bores heads his wife she gave
As well in Wales is knowne,
A lyon at his feete doth lye,
At head a dragon greene :
More things who lists to search with eye,
On tombe may well be seene.

No. I ?
In the window now he lyes.

Amid the church Lord Hastings lay
Lord Aborgaynie then :
And since his death remov'd away,
By fine device of man :
And layd within a windowe right,
Full flat on stonie wall,
Where now he doth in open sight
Remaine to people all.
The window is well made and wrought,
A costly worke to see :
In which his noble armes are thought
Of purpose there to bee.
A ragged sleeve and sixe red birds
Is pourtrayd in the glasse ;
His wife hath there her left arme bare,
It seems her sleeve it was
That hangs about his necke full fine,
Right ore a purple weede,
A robe of that same colour too
The ladie wears indeede,
Under his legges a lyon red ;
His armes are rare and ritch
A harrold that could shewe them welle
Can blase not many sitch.
Sixe lyons white, the ground fayro blew,
Three flower-de-luces gold

The ground of them is red of hew
And goodly to behold.
But note a greater matter now
Upon his tombe in stone

<small>Some say this great Lord was called Bruce and not Hastings, but most doe hold opinion he was called Hastings.</small>

Were fourteene lords that knees did bow
Unto this lord alone.
Of this rare worke a porch is made
The barrons there remaine,
In good old stone and auncient trade
To shew all ages plaine,
What homage was to Hastings due,
What honor he did win,
What armes he gave, and so to blaze
What Lord had Hastings bin.
Right ore against this windowe loe

<small>No. VIII.
A Ladie of Abergaynie.</small>

In stone a ladie lyes ;
And in her hands a hart I troe,
She holds before your eyes,
And on her breast a great fayre shield,
In which she beares no more
But three great flower-de-luces large ;
And even loe, right ore
Her head another ladie lyes

<small>No. VII.
A ladie of some noble house whose name I know not.</small>

With squirrell on her hand,
And at her feete in stone likewise
A couching hound doth stand :
They say her squirrell lept away,
And toward it she run ;
And as from fall she sought to stay
The little pretie bun,
Right downe from top of wall she fell
And tooke her death thereby,
This what I heard, I doe you tell
And what is seene with eye.

<small>No. X.
Doctor Lewis lately judge of he Amoraltie.</small>

A friend of myne who lately dyed
That Doctor Lewis hight,
Within that church his tombe I spyed
Well wrought and fayre to sight.
O Lord (quoth I) we all must dye,
No lawe, nor learning's lore,
No judgement deepe nor knowledge hye,
No riches lesse or more ;
No office, place, nor calling great,
No worldly pompe at all,
Can keepe us from the mortall threat,
Of death when God doth call.
Sith none of these good gifts on earth,
Have power to make us live,
And no good fortune from our birth,
No hower of breath can give.
Thinke not on life and pleasure heere,
They passe like beames of sunne :
For nought from hence we carrie cleere,
When man his race hath runne.

NOTE.—The numbers refer to the different Monuments in the order in which they are described.

THE MONUMENTS.

We now come to the consideration of the Monumental Effigies themselves, which have been admirably illustrated by a beautiful series of photographs, numbered from I to XIII. Many years ago they were most accurately and exquisitely drawn by my esteemed friend Edward Blore, Esq., the distinguished architect, who paid much attention to them; and it is greatly to be regretted that his most beautiful drawings of Monumental Effigies have never been published, for they form the most complete and valuable series ever made. As these effigies are so intimately connected with the church in which they are, and of which they form part, it will be desirable to say a few words concerning it and what appears to be its history. The Priory, as has been stated, was founded in the beginning of the XIII century, and there was of course a church or chapel belonging to it, which must have been in the Norman style of architecture of the period. It was probably not very large and perhaps of rude execution. It was a common practice to take down, alter, enlarge, and rebuild these churches as the conventual community advanced in importance and wealth, and these improvements were often the result of special benefactions. It is very likely therefore that something of the kind took place here, for from the style of the tower, transepts, choir, aisles, and chancel, this present structure appears to have been erected in the early part of the XIV century. There are now no appreciable remains of the original Norman architecture, though there seem to have been formerly traces of an archway in one transept. This church was cruciform, with a central tower, eastwards of which was the monks' choir, with its twenty-four stalls, twelve on each side, of carved oak of the XIV century, which remain to the present time: and Richard Symonds in his diary states that at the time of his visit in 1645, there was "A very faire roode loft and old organs," but does not say in what part of the church. The transepts were extended eastward by the erection of aisles opening into the choir, and these aisles seem to have been used as burial places first of the Lords of Abergavenny, and subsequently of other great notable personages of the district; the south aisle having acquired the name of the Herbert Chapel, and the north that of the Lewis Aisle or Chapel. The choir and chancel are of great length, and it is possible there may have been a Lady Chapel beyond the High Altar, seeing that the church was dedicated to the blessed Virgin Mary.

Repairs and alterations have doubtless been made in the church at various periods. The pavement of the Herbert Chapel seems at one time to have been considerably raised, so as to bury the bases of all the monuments, and to build up the lower portion of a doorway which led from the chapel into the Priory. In 1828 very extensive alterations and repairs were made. The south transept was parted off from the Herbert Chapel and converted into a vestry, the floor was raised many feet, by which operation one monument against the south wall, and several slabs are said to lie buried beneath it. A school was also for some time held in the vestry, and the boys having access to the Herbert Chapel, have sadly contributed to the injury and disfigurment of the monuments by cutting their initials all over the figures, and perhaps breaking off and carrying away many portions. But there must have been at some earlier period a great systematic and more violent destruction of the tombs, of which we have no record. The tombs were certainly perfect at the time of Churchyard's visit at the end of the XVI century, (and indeed as late as the visit of Richard Symonds in 1645,) though he certainly mentions that one had been removed, and not only the tombs remained but also the stained glass in the windows, displaying sundry coats of arms; some of these however appear to have been lost or destroyed in 1828 during the alterations in the Church. The most probable time of this destruction was the period of the Rebellion, when sad destruction of Monuments and other objects in churches was committed by the soldiers of the Commonwealth throughout the land. At some subsequent period such of the fragments as could be found seem to have been collected and fitted together so as to make up the tombs again, and it is difficult to determine whether the various parts so refitted really belonged to them, or formed a portion of the reredos of some destroyed altar, as many of the figures of saints and holy persons have special allusion to the Virgin Mary.

These Monuments are chiefly in the form of altar tombs, or tombs in recesses, having recumbent effigies of the deceased lying upon them, which were intended for accurate portraits. Monuments of this kind were occasionally erected by parties during their lifetime, blanks being left in the inscription to be filled up with the date when the person should die, which in some cases was never done, and the blanks still remain. These recumbent figures are thought to have had their origin from the practice in early times of making effigies in wax or other material of great personages to represent them as nearly as possible as when living; they were used and carried at their funerals, and may have been placed for some time on their graves, and subsequently replaced by figures in stone.

No. I.

GEORGE DE CANTELUPE?

The most ancient of these Knightly Effigies is a wooden figure carved in oak, and though it has been but little cared for, is perhaps the most interesting of the series; for these wooden Effigies are not common, and I have little doubt that I shall be able to identify the individual. The Effigy represents a very young man of slender and graceful frame and handsome countenance. He is habited in his full suit of armour, reclining on his back, as laid out in death, with his hands raised in prayer on his breast, and his feet resting on a lion. The calm and easy pose of the figure, and the mild and placid expression of the features, which together with all the accessories of the various parts of the armour are most carefully executed, shew that it was the work of no mean hand, and that there were statuary artists of much talent and skill in those days; and this figure gives reason for believing the Effigy to be a faithful portrait of the individual it represents, for the eyes are wide open, thus shewing that it was not intended to represent a corpse, but a living man, though in that posture; and it is by no means improbable that it was the Effigy used at his funeral, and subsequently placed on his grave or tomb. The features are small, regular, and youthful, and there is no appearance of any trace of moustache or beard. The aperture in the hood of mail shewing the face is five inches and three-fourths long and four and a half wide, and the figure is five feet nine inches from the crown of the head to the bottom of the heel. The head rests on two cushions, the upper being placed diagonally on the lower; the left leg is crossed over the right; the feet are perfect, and rest on a boldly carved lion, whose head however has long been wanting.

The figure is habited in a hauberk and hood of chain mail, which though the rings are not marked on the wood is most perfectly indicated by the very careful manner in which the folds or rather the set of the armour is shewn at the neck and sleeves; and with such care has this been attended to, that the swell of the chain mail over the ears is most accurately given; the rings of the mail would appear marked on the colour with which the figure was covered. Round the coif at the temples is a narrow band or fillet, which was probably gilt. The sleeves terminate at the wrists, and are edged with a fillet. The hands from the slenderness of the fingers seem to be uncovered, but if they represent gloves of mail the fingers of them are divided. Over the hauberk is the sleveless surcoat, which is open partly up the front for the convenience of riding, and the folds of it are arranged in a very graceful and artistic manner. This surcoat is confined at the waist by a narrow strap-like belt fastened by a small buckle, and the end passing through a sliding loop falls down in front. Below this the sword belt crosses the figure in a slanting direction; it is about three inches broad, and is fastened with a buckle in front,—the end of it after passing through the buckle, being turned back behind the hilt of the sword, hangs down on the left side, and shews the metal ornaments at the end of it. The sword and hilt have unfortunately been broken away, and all that remains is the cross guard and the loop attached to the belt, through which the scabbard passed as its support, and which is shewn by a small row of studs, which clearly points out how this loop formed part of the belt. The legs are clothed with chausses of chain mail, and above the knees the thighs appear to be covered with chaussons which terminate at the knee with genouillères of plate. The spurs are the single short prick spur of the time. These are mentioned by Gough as having been gilt, and originally the whole Effigy was finely coated with gesso, and painted in its proper colours, for small traces of colour still remain in parts, especially at the under folds of the surcoat, which shew that it was of a bright red colour; and there is no doubt that the fillet round the head and wrists, the spurs and ornamental parts of the sword and belt were gilt. These particular details of the armour, compared with other effigies of known date, as well as from what is also certainly known of the armour at particular periods, indicate the date of this figure as of the latter part of the XIII century, and would fix it about 1275.

Churchyard does not mention any wooden figure, and the earliest notice of it seems to be by Rd. Symonds in 1645. He describes the window thus:—"North window, old : the borders are : gules, three fleurs-de-lis or; a maunch gules; and Valance; his coate, and azure, six lions rampant argent." He then adds a sketch of the shield with the three fleurs-de-lis, which are the Cantelupe coat. "At the bottome of the window lies a statue in wood; two cushions under his head, crosse-legd, a loose coate and belt. They call him the builder of the Church." This seems to identify it with the figure mentioned by Churchyard in his day, as "Layd within a window, right, full flat on stonie wall." It was seen in 1646 by the author of the manuscript as given in Gough's Camden, which Coxe quotes, and calls it "the recumbent effigies of a man coarsely carved in wood." The author of the M.S. in question thus describes it:—" In a window in an isle of the North end of the Quire of the said Church is there a very ould Monument of Irish Oake, lying cross legged, the left leg uppermost, crossing the right with gilt spurs on. On his armour his surcoat, but there is neither any expression of Arms or Crest. Who's it is I could not learn, most probably one of the ancient Lords of Abergavenny, for in the window over him, in the border of the window is Valence, for they have been anciently Lords of Abergavenny likewise." It is to be regretted that no traces of armorial bearings now exist in any of the windows, but it is not at all necessary that the arms in the window should have belonged to this effigy, which was never fixed there, but was in all probability only placed up aloft on the window sill out of the way, no one knowing anything about it, and having no settled resting place of its own, has remained there ever since; for its date is earlier than the present Church, which is of the XIV century; and seems to be of the Hastings period; and it is most probable that to its having been so put aloft out of harm's way, we are indebted for its preservation; for notwithstanding the lapse of six centuries, there is little appearance of wanton injury. It must be remarked that the figure and the bed on which it lies are of one block of wood, and that the body of the figure is roughly hollowed out. The head seems to have cracked when newly made, and a piece of wood has been skilfully inserted to fill up the flaw, which was concealed under the painting.

Having now ascertained the date of the effigy, the next step will be to endeavour to identify it with the person whom it was intended to represent. When we look to the series of the Lords of Abergavenny, and to the period to which this figure belongs, we find one with whom it accords in every particular, viz:—George de Cantelupe, Lord of Abergavenny, who died in the year of 1273, at the age of twenty. The youthful figure and countenance of the Effigy are so exactly suited to that age, and the time of his death coincides so precisely with the date indicated by the characteristics of the armour, as I think to leave no reasonable doubt that this figure is the representation and portrait of George de Cantelupe, who was the son of William de Cantelupe and Eva, the daughter of William de Braose, and heiress in her own right of the Lordship of Abergavenny. The arms of Cantelupe were gules, three fleurs-de-lis or—and would have been emblazoned on the surcoat in proper colours, and the actual red colour of the surcoat as shewn by the remains of the paint which are still to be seen on the under part where it is protected from injury, is just the colour of the surcoat which a Cantelupe would have worn with the three large fleurs-de-lis emblazoned on his breast, and is a strong confirmation of my supposition. His father died in 1256, and his mother Eva, of whom we shall speak hereafter, in 1257, when he succeeded as heir to the Lordship, being then a minor of only four years of age. He was born at Abergavenny on Good Friday, 1253, 36th of Henry III, and died on St. Mark's Day, 25th April, 1273, at the age of twenty. Although so young he had married the daughter of Edmond Lacy, Earl of Lincoln, but having only one son who died during his lifetime, he left no issue, and was the last of the line of Cantelupe who held the Lordship of Abergavenny.

Before proceeding to the other Monuments it may not be out of place to make some observations on these wooden effigies, several of which are to be found in different Churches in various parts of the country. The subject is somewhat new, and not altogether devoid of interest, and will serve to illustrate the figure of which we have been treating. The most celebrated of the wooden figures is perhaps that in Gloucester Cathedral, generally considered to be the Monument of Robert Curthose, Duke of Normandy, son of William the Conqueror. At Bareham in Norfolk, in the North aisle of the Church, under an arch in the wall, there is one which the arms bespeak to be the Effigy of Sir Hugh Bardolph, who died 1203 ; it is described as a cumbent statue of wood, cut out of the same piece of wood on which it lies, but some of the smaller or more salient parts were made separately and fastened to the rest with wooden pins. The whole is hollow and open at the bottom. It was originally painted all over but is now almost bare. This is exactly the description of our effigy here. At Clifton Reynes in Buckinghamshire, are four wooden effigies, two knights and two ladies. One knight and one lady being separate figures lie beside each other within a canopied recess of the decorated period in the chancel aisle. The figures, however, from the armour and costume of the lady, are of the XIII century, that of the knight is assigned to Simon de Borard, who died 1267. The other two lie side by side on a stone altar tomb which stands beneath the archway between the chapel and the aisle. The costume and armour of the knight, and the costume of the lady indicate a later date, and the history of the parish attributes it to Ralph de Reynes who died about 1310, with which date the armour and shields of arms agree. "The effigies are hollow and unconnected with the slabs on which they rest; they have been deeply scooped out and the cavity left in a rough and a jagged state. There is no certainty that any of them occupy their original position." That is just the case with ours. These Monuments have been minutely described in the Archæological Journal for 1854, Vol. XI.

These wooden Effigies seem to have prevailed during the XIII century. Robert Curthose would appear to be an exception, but it is very possible that they may have been used earlier, although we have now not any of a very early date. It has however been thought questionable whether that of Robert Curthose is really his Effigy, although it has for centuries passed under his name. He died 1134, and certainly the armour of the figure does not at all correspond in detail with that represented on the seals of the Royal and other great personages who were his contemporaries, but it does exactly with the known armour of the XIII century. It has however undergone serious misadventures, for Sandford who saw it describes it, and has given an engraving of it as it was in 1665, and he tells us that "the rebellious soldiers of the Parliamentary Army tore it to pieces, but the parcels thereof ready to be burnt were by the care of Sir Humphrey Tracy bought of the soldiers and privately laid up till the restoration of His Majesty Charles II, when the old pieces put together again, were repaired and beautified with gold and colours at the charge of that worthy person." This seems to have been done in anticipation of a Restoration, which is rather a curious circumstance, and it is in vain to speculate on what sort of a renovation of the figure from the fragments took place, beautified with gold and colours as it has since been, without a close examination of the wooden structure of the figure, which now looks like a knight of the XIII century. Rowelled spurs of the XIV century have been added. The coronet seems also part of the later restoration. This history may account for the figure as it now is, not corresponding with the period of his death.

A question arises as to the use of these wooden figures, whether they were originally intended as sepulchral Monuments like the stone coffin lids and effigies of cross-legged knights of the same period. It was the custom in early times, on the death of great personages, to prepare an effigy of the deceased to be arrayed like him and carried in the procession at the state funeral, and the impression on my mind at one time was that they were originally prepared for such state ceremony; but the care and pains taken in the sculpture, painting, gilding, and decoration of them is hardly compatible with the haste required in the preparation of a funeral, and I am therefore disposed to think that they were designed for more permanent Monumental Effigies or portraits, being very carefully and skilfully prepared so as to exclude all idea of haste; and when we consider the very beautiful Monument in Westminster Abbey of William de Valence, who died 1296, which consists of a recumbent figure of carved oak, cased in plates of gilt-copper richly and beautifully ornamented with enamel, there can I think be little doubt that they were intended for ornamental Monuments, and that when from age and cleaning they had become shabby, and the colours and gilding worn away, they were often removed from their original sites, and either destroyed or stowed away in some less important position, and there not being on them any name, or inscription, or other means of identification, it was forgotten whom they represented, and no further interest was taken in them; and that may have been the case with this effigy, when at some time prior to the visit of Churchyard it had been moved from the middle of the church, and all certain knowledge of the person it was intended to represent having passed away, it was put aside on the sill of a window, with which probably it had no connexion, and was no longer heeded. The wood was once coated with fine plaster on which links of the mail were moulded, and the whole richly painted in the proper colours and gilt. These effigies therefore must have been brilliant and beautiful objects when newly made, and the enamelled monument of de Valence in Westminister Abbey was therefore only a more permanent and costly exemplification of the style then prevailing.

It is evident that these wooden effigies were not chance pieces of work, for there is one peculiarity which pervades them all wherever they are found, and seems to shew that they were systematically constructed. They are always made as portraits with the eyes open. They are always hollow, the block of wood which forms the body being roughly scooped out. There must have been some reason for this. The object may have been to render the figures as light as possible when they were to be moved about, but it was most probably done to prevent the effigy from splitting or cracking, which might have been the case from the more speedy drying of the wood at the surface, when there was a large block of less dry wood within, which would prevent any internal shrinkage, and this the excavation of the block would tend to prevent; to have dressed a simple lay figure in armour would certainly have made a very heavy and inconvenient object, and its weight would have made it very unwieldly, and liable to shift from its position when transported and moved about, whereas that inconvenience would hardly have been felt when the figure was only arrayed in light robes, and might itself have been of lighter construction. Therefore for an effigy clad in chain mail, a firm carved wooden figure properly coloured, would have been found in every respect more convenient than one dressed in loose chain armour, and might afterwards have served for a Monumental effigy for a great length of time.

As a matter cognate to, and illustrative of the subject in hand, it may not be amiss to say something respecting ancient state funerals, and the effigies of the deceased persons used on those occasions, inasmuch as the effigies on the altar tombs seem to have been suggested by those employed at the funerals, and to have been made after them as permanent portraits of the deceased. For obvious reasons the actual bodies of deceased persons could not generally have been exposed to public view. In many cases it would have been impossible, though I believe in cases where circumstances required, or would admit of it, the actual body was occasionally laid out arrayed in the habits which he wore, and exposed to view, perhaps to afford evidence of his death, or to gratify the feelings of fond relations and friends, and possibly to satisfy a morbid curiosity of persons in general; and so the corpse lay in state, guarded and watched by various attendants for a short time before it was coffined, and this was most probably the origin of "lying in state." The usual practice, however, with persons of very high distinction, was very soon after death to disembowel and embalm the body, (the heart being buried in an urn in one place, and the bowels sometimes in another), sometimes salting in, wrapping it closely in cere cloth, or casing it in lead, and enclosing it in a chest or coffin. An effigy of the deceased was speedily prepared, formed of wood, the face and hands being carefully carved and coated with fine plaster or wax, so modelled and tinted as to be an exact portrait of the defunct person. This seems to have been arrayed in the richest dress or robes of state which the person was entitled to wear, in order to shew his state and degree.

These Effigies being prepared in portraiture of the deceased produced the same effect as if the actual corpse were carried in the funeral procession, and was placed under the herse in the church. As they were carried on the coffin which contained the body, that may be considered as represented by the altar tomb, and the sculptured figure lying thereon as holding the place of the funeral effigy. The wooden figure of Robert Curthose in Gloucester Cathedral still lies on an ornamented oaken chest which may be well considered to represent the coffin. In the beautiful enamelled Monument of William de Valence, the effigy also reposes on a wooden chest, enriched with enamelled metal plates.

A short account of a few great funerals taken from Gough's sepulchral Monuments, will serve to shew how these effigies were used, and how important a part they played in the state ceremonial. At the funeral of Richard, Duke of York, father of Edward the IV, who died 1460, it is stated "he was taken and placed in the choir of the church within a herse garnished very richly." "He was upon the herse *in portraiture*, the face uncovered, the hands joined, clothed in a mantle of pers (that is of a grey colour), furred with ermine, on his head a cap of maintenance of purple velvet, furred with ermine."

At the interment of Edward IV, "The body after it was cered was laid in the Chapel of St. Stephen, at Westminster for eight days, and was conveyed into the Abbey of Westminster, having on it a large black cloth of gold, with a cross of silver. In the herse in Westminster Abbey, above the body and cloth of gold was *the figure of the King*, royally habited. A Royal Crown on his head, a Sceptre in one hand, and in the other a Ball of silver gilt with a cross patée."

Of Henry VII—"Dying at Richmond, his body was brought into the Great Chamber, and rested three days, and the same in the Hall and Chapel. On Wednesday, the 9th May, 1509, it was conveyed in a chair, (car?), covered with black cloth of gold, garnished with escocheons of fine gold, with his effigies over it apparrelled in rich robes, the crown on his head, and the Sceptre and gilt Ball in his hands."

"Queen Elizabeth of York, consort of Henry VII, died at the Tower in 1503; after being embalmed the corpse was conveyed into a chair, whose sides and coffer were covered with white velvet, with a cross of white cloth of gold, well fringed, and an image or person dressed like the Queen in her very robes of estate, her very rich Crown upon her head, her hair about her shoulders, her Sceptre in her right hand, and her fingers well garnished with rings of gold and precious stones."

Henry VIII.—"On the 14th day of February, 1547, about ten in the morning, the King's body set forward towards Windsor, in a state charriot, *his Effigies* lying upon the coffin, with the true Imperial Crown on the head, and under it a nightcap of black satin, set full of precious stones, and apparelled in robes of crimson velvet, furred with miniver, powdered with ermine. The Collar of the Garter with the Order of St. George about the neck, a crimson satin doublet, embroidered with gold, two bracelets about the wrists set with stones and pearl, a fair arming sword by his side, the Sceptre in his right hand, the Ball in his left, a pair of scarlet hose and crimson velvet shoes, gloves on the hands, and several diamond rings on the fingers, drawn by eight great horses, trapped with black, adorned with escocheons, and a shafferoon on their heads, on each of which rode a child of honour carrying a bannerol of the King's arms. Thus with exceeding great train of four miles in length the body was conveyeth to Syon, where it was received at the church door by the Bishops of London, Bristol, and Gloucester, who performed Dirge that night, and next morning the corpse being brought into the church, was placed in a herse like that at Whitehall, but the effigies was conveyed into the vestry."

Edward VI.—"A chariot covered with cloth of gold, tissued with silver, carried the King's corpse with the King's picture from Whitehall to Westminster, where it was placed under a stately herse."

Queen Mary.—"Her body being embalmed, was put into a coffin enclosed in lead, covered with purple velvet, which at the time of the funeral was put in a chariot, having thereupon the representation of the Queen, and so they solemnly proceeded to the Abbey of Westminster."

Queen Elizabeth.—At her funeral there was "a lively picture of Her Majesty's whole body in her Parliament robes, with a crown on her head, and a sceptre in her hand, lying on the corpse enshrined in lead and balmed, borne in a chariot, drawn by four horses trapt in black velvet;" and so it was conveyed with great solemnity to Westminster Abbey, 28 April, 1602. A detailed drawing of this procession is given in the Vetusta Monumenta, Vol. III, and there the effigy is shewn lying on the coffin exactly as here described, and just so is the figure of the Queen represented on her monument in Henry VII's Chapel, lying beneath a stately canopy, which may well be considered as the monumental representative of the funeral herse used at the ceremony.

James I died at Theobald's, 27 March, 1625—and "the body was for greater state conveyed by torchlight to Denmark House," the Queen's new Palace in the Strand, which before her death in 1618, she had greatly enlarged and beautified, and which though before called Somerset House, the King had ordered to be called Denmark House. Here it rested from the 13th April to the 7th May, when it was "carried to Westminster Abbey to a stately herse, and interred in the Chapel of Henry VII." An engraving of this herse is given in Sandford, and there is seen an effigy of the King, arrayed in his royal robes with the crown on his head, and a sceptre and orb in his hands. James I. has no monument erected to his memory, and he was, I believe, the last of the Sovereigns of England, whose effigy was prepared and carried at the funeral ; and at this time the practise of erecting stately architectural canopies over altar tombs bearing monumental effigies seems to have ceased. The funeral of Charles the II. was private. At the funeral of Queen Mary II, the coffin was placed under a rich herse or mausoleum in Westminster Abbey, but only the crown, sceptre, and orb were placed on the coffin.

The wooden forms of many of these effigies still exist in Westminster

Abbey, and by the kind permission of the Dean, I was enabled to inspect them. Dart in his History of Westminster Abbey, 1723, describes them as being then in a broken and tattered condition, and "stripp'd of their robes which he supposes to have been done by the late rebels." They were then kept in wainscoat presses as they are now, and are very unsightly objects, for the state robes and clothes having been removed after the funerals, they are now like great jointed dolls much broken; the faces, however, of all have been most carefully carved, and reminded me by their work and style very much of our wooden effigy in the Priory Church. Their eyes are all open, and they are evidently intended as portraits of living persons, and I at once recognised in one the features of Henry VII. The faces and hands of these figures, unless they wore gloves, were coated with wax prepared and tinted to represent life, like the figures of that distinguished artist Madame Tussaud, who has simply perpetuated an art which has been practised in this country for centuries. A similar exhibition I remember to have seen in Fleet-street, upwards of sixty years ago, in which was a celebrated figure of the old witch Mother Shipton, which by an ingenious arrangement of a board in the floor in front of the figure, on any one approaching her, threw out her foot, and greeted them with a kick on the shin.

In early times state funerals were under the direction of the heralds and the clergy, who were great adepts in the arts, and especially in matters of ceremonial and decoration. These effigies when they were arrayed in royal robes and jewels, were of course carefully dismantled after the funeral ceremonies, but when the dresses and decorations were only " furnished " by those who " undertook " to " perform funerals," they were frequently laid aside and preserved in the church, and this was particularly the case in Westminster Abbey, where many grand state funerals took place, and there was space for their preservation. They were put in glass cases, and this is the origin of the wax works which were formerly exhibited in the Abbey. Several of these figures still remain in these cases, though dirty, faded, and tattered from age. The figure of Queen Elizabeth is described by Dart as being stripped in 1723. It was, however, re-dressed for a special occasion in the last century, and I have no doubt that the wooden block is the identical one which was prepared and carried at her funeral obsequies.

With regard to the exposition of the actual body after death, I will relate what I myself witnessed in the year 1828, at Rome, where ancient customs are or were very long continued. I was there in the early part of that year, and the Carnival was to commence on the 9th of February. A Cardinal who had died the previous day was to be buried at the church of Ara Cœli, which is close to the Capitol, on the morning of that same day. This ceremony had to be got over early, as the solemnity of the funeral, and the noisy gaiety of the Carnival were incompatible in such close proximity at the same moment. When I reached the church I found the funeral obsequies were over, the Pope and Cardinals who assisted at the ceremony having been there early in the morning. The church was hung all over with draperies and festoons of black and gold. The seats of their Eminences covered with black cloth, and the throne of his Holiness of purple and gold, were placed in front of the altar. In the middle of the church, on a highly elevated and inclined bed, which was covered with cloth of gold, bordered with black velvet, embroidered in gold, surrounded with one hundred large tapers lay the corpse of the deceased Cardinal, arrayed in his episcopal vestments of purple and silver, having his mitra preciosa on his head, which rested on a cushion of purple velvet, and his pastoral staff lying by his side. His countenance was very placid and composed, and being a handsome man of middle age, his profile was remarkably fine, and if my memory rightly serves me, the cheeks were slightly tinged with rouge to take off the ghastly paleness of death. The figure presented precisely the appearance of those early episcopal monuments which we see in our cathedrals; and the impression on my mind has ever since been that these monuments were intended to represent the Bishop as he lay in state after his death. It was the custom to leave the funeral effigies on or near the grave for some time after the funeral ceremony, and I am disposed to consider the altar tomb as representing the coffin, the sculptured recumbent statue, the effigy lying upon it, and the beautiful canopies erected over so many fine altar tombs as representing the gorgeous herses or catafalques which were set up in the churches, and under which the coffins with the effigies upon them were placed during the performance of the funeral ceremonies.

No. II.

SIR WILLIAM HASTINGS?

We now come to the consideration of the Monuments marked II and III in the photographic illustrations, and as they are contemporary with each other they may be grouped together. They are sculptured in freestone, the material of which such permanent Monumental Effigies were usually made during the XIII and XIV centuries. Such stone is not found in any part of this district, and as it is hardly probable that in so remote a part of the country, and in so small a place as Abergavenny then was, there were artists capable of executing such a piece of sculpture, the artists must have come from a distance, and it is very probable that the entire monuments, or at least the effigies were brought from some other region to be erected here. It is difficult to say from what exact place the stone came, but it was probably from Dundry, as it is quite certain from documents in my possession that large quantities of freestone from the Dundry quarries were brought to Newport in 1447 and 1448 for the repair or rebuilding part of the castle. An examination of the armour will shew us that their age is about the middle of the XIV century, and first of No. II.

This occupies the lower part of the recess of a window which has been filled in with stone panelling of decorated architecture of later date than that of the chapel. It consists of a recumbent figure of a knight in armour, reclining rather on his left side, his face, which is seen through the opening in the armour, being turned towards the spectator, and as the eyes are wide open, it is evident that it is not intended to represent a man as laid out in death; it must therefore be considered to be a likeness of the person to be commemorated, and seems to represent a man of at least thirty years of age. The features have a fat swollen appearance and the expression is not pleasing. There is no appearance of moustache on the upper lip. By the head of the figure, joined to the wall, stands a small semi-octagonal pedestal, ten inches wide and six inches deep, the use of which is not obvious, unless it served as a support for the helm as sketched by Symonds, and for that purpose it would appear to have been very small if the helm was of full size. The figure is a very good piece of sculpture, and the attitude graceful and easy, but it has unfortunately been very seriously mutilated and then roughly repaired, some fragments being fitted up together, and vacancies filled up with common mortar or plaster, so as to preserve the general character of an armed figure, which work is concealed as far as appearance goes by the frequent coats of coloured wash it has received, and which I should like to remove were I not apprehensive of disclosing more mischief than we could afterwards conceal, without revealing anything that would be of service.

The figure is six feet six inches in length from the point of the bascinet to the bottom of the heel. The head rests on a single cushion, the ends of which are brought to a point and terminated in a tassel. It is armed with a bascinet and camail of banded mail, which descends to and lies on the shoulders like a tippet, and exhibits well the opening for the face and the mode of attaching the chain mail to the bascinet by means of staples which pass through the plate, and are kept in their position by a lace which runs through their loops. The body was clad in a hauberk of banded mail, which is visible at the arm holes, over which is a sleeveless jupon, or close fitting surcoat of quilted or embroidered material as appears at the folds at the sides, which reached halfway down the thighs and had a border of fur round the bottom. The shoulders are guarded with epauliéres of two plates which appear from beneath the camail, and the arms are encased in plate armour, having coudiéres with roundels at the elbow joints. The body and right arm have sustained much injury, and have been clumsily repaired; and there was probably a shield on the breast as mentioned by Churchyard. The left hand is gone, the right side of the body and the right arm with it, and this is just where the shield should have been, the left hand holding the strap. All this has been broken away, and the arm and body made good with common mortar or plaster well coated with the usual colouring. The right hand grasps the hilt of his dagger, and wears a gauntlet of plate with separate fingers, the overlapping plates of which may be felt. The chaussons are of studded work, which may have represented leather, or pourpointerie attached by studs to metal splints underneath; to these are attached the genouilliéres or knee pieces of plate, which terminate in a fringe of some material. The legs are cased in plate, and the feet which are too much broken to determine exactly their covering, rest on an animal with long legs and tail, said by Churchyard and Symonds to be a greyhound, then probably more perfect and less clogged with colour than now. The knightly belt encircled the body at the hips, and was of rich work, being ornamented with quatrefoils in square panels, and four-leaved flowers set cornerwise, alternating with each other, which would have been of Goldsmith's work. The sword lies by the left side, and had a cross hilt, and the scabbard like that of the dagger is ornamented with a band of small quatrefoils by which it was attached to the belt, but the connexion is now broken away. The effigy fills up the whole of the recess, and the right leg is crossed over the left in an easy posture to suit the arrangement of the figure, without having any other significance. Of this Monument Symonds says "In the south window of the same chappel a statue cross-legged. This stands up right at his head;" and here he gives a rough and hasty sketch of a helmet, such as was worn at jousts and in battle in the XIV century; the form is somewhat cylindrical, and there is a narrow horizontal opening opposite the eyes; the upper part is encircled by a coronet, above which rises something of a conical form, the top of which seems to be broken off, but whether it is intended to represent the top of the helm, or the base of a crest issuing from the coronet, it is not possible to say. Churchyard speaks of a "sleeve in top and crest;" but how a sleeve, which is only a piece of drapery could form a crest it is not easy to see. The coronet is like the crowns represented on the helms of sovereigns or royal princes, but there is no royal prince or personage whom it could represent, as an examination of Sandford's Genealogical History will shew; it is therefore most probably a coronet out of which the crest issued, and as the Hastings crest is a bull's head erased, gorged with a ducal coronet, it is very likely that was represented here, the cone being part of the bull's neck, and this will be in favour of its being a Hastings monument. Symonds further says, "A greyhound at his feet. Dyed because he killed his greyhound say they."

The identification of this monument with the person who lies buried here has always been a matter of much difficulty, and it is somewhat presumptuous in me to attempt to solve that which has puzzled many others much more learned in such matters who have turned their attention to the subject. The monument itself supplies us with no information except the date of the armour, which refers it to the middle of the XIV century. Had that been all, there would have been little difficulty, though without any actual proof, in attributing it to the gallant knight Sir William Hastings, illegitimate son of John, Lord Hastings, and so half brother of Lawrence Hastings, Lord of Abergavenny, who being much attached to his half-brother, granted him several manors, and among them Castle Arnold, where he is supposed to have resided. Sir William died unmarried 1349. Churchyard has, however, given us an account of some armorial bearings which in his day were apparent on the monument, but his knowledge of heraldry was perhaps not great, and his mode of describing them so puzzling and unintelligible, possibly owing to the necessities of his rhymes, that he has thrown additional perplexity into the matter; he says

> "His shield of black he bears on brest,
> A white crowe plain thereon,
> A ragged sleeve in top and crest
> All wrought in goodly stone."

With the kind aid of a valued friend who is very learned in heraldic matters, I shall hope to be able to offer some solution of the enigma. No such coat as sa, a crow argent is known to have been borne by any family at that time, and it may even be doubted if there was such a coat. He may have been mistaken in his bird, which might have been a falcon or a dove, but which he has called a crow; but that will not help us to identify the bearer. The "ragged sleeve" or maunch certainly points to Hastings as if he were one of that family, the arms of Hastings being or, a maunch gules. But what is the meaning of "in top and crest?" It is well known that in those days the crest was never borne but on the top of the heaume or helm, and in that case it would have been on the heaume underneath the head of the effigy; but there is no heaume as the head rests on a cushion, so that the word crest does not apply to the monument, at least as it now is, and was probably only introduced to supply a rhyme for "brest." It is therefore not clear that the maunch or ragged sleeve was a crest on a helm at all; and it might very probably have been in the arms, on a chief on a canton, and so have been at the upper part or "in top" of the shield, and is favourable to the supposition that the effigy represents a Hastings, though he may have been illegitimate. The bend sinister or baton was not then the general mark of bastardy. The arms of such illegitimate sons as had any were variously composed of portions of their father's arms; sometimes the arms of their father were borne on a bend or a fess. I therefore consider it very possible that when Sir William Hastings was made a knight, he may have obtained a coat of arms of his own, and that the arms of his father may have been placed on a canton or on a chief, either of which would have been at the upper part of the shield, and so would explain Churchyard's expression "in top," and indicate his connexion with the family of Hastings, and in that case the coat might well be sa, a crow, or any other bird argent, with the Hastings coat in chief or canton; and as he died without issue, his coat, as it began with him would also cease with him, and would therefore never appear as the coat of any family. In the marginal note to the poem it is stated that the window and other parts about him shew that he was a stranger, but we are not told what these indications were. He certainly was not a Lord of Abergavenny, and so might have been considered a stranger in that chapel, and the different coat of arms on his shield might have caused him to have been so considered at a later period, when all about the early monuments seems to have been forgotten. Churchyard, however, makes a further perplexing statement; he says "Three gold lyons gay, and nine flower-de-luces his arms doth full display;" and in the margin he says "Blewe is the label whereon are nyne flower-de-luces." He however omits to state where these arms are, whether on the tomb or in the window. This coat points to royalty, the three lyons being the royal arms of England, and the label of three points, charged with nine fleurs-de-lis being the royal mark of Cadency, indicating the arms of the Earls of Lancaster. It cannot possibly be any member or connexion of the royal house, for Sandford gives a most minute account of every member of the royal line, male and female; it is therefore not possible that the knight represented should be one of royal extraction or connexion. It is very possible that the arms of the Earls of Lancaster may have appeared in the window glass without having any relation to the monument below. The Earls of Lancaster had manors, castles, and estates in that part of the country, and it is by no means improbable that he may have been a knight in the service of the Earl of Lancaster, and thus his arms might have been introduced into the window as those of the patron and chief under whom the knight served who was buried below. Having taken all these various circumstances into consideration, I feel strongly disposed to assign this monument to Sir William Hastings, as the most probable personage to whom it can be attributed, although it is not possible to pronounce with any certainty.

No. III.

LAWRENCE DE HASTINGS.

This Monument is of freestone, and is certainly of that of an important personage. It is an altar tomb, on the upper slab of which lies the recumbent effigy of a knight in armour of the XIV century. It stands between the main piers, under the archway which divides the aisle, or Herbert Chapel as it is called, from the original choir of the monastery, and close against the back of the panelling of the stalls. This tomb has been very ill-used, having been intruded upon by the monument of William Baker, erected in the XVII century, which has been built close up against the head of it, and to make room for which the slab bearing the effigy has been forced forward, and so made to overhang the tomb by eight inches, and thus the slab with the figure is made to look as if it did not belong to it. Both tomb and figure are so close against the oak panelling that it is not possible to see the other side of either. In the alterations which this part of the church has undergone by the raising of the pavement, the base of the monument has been buried. The altar tomb is one of very good decorated character of the middle of the XIV century. The sides consist of a series of five niches with projecting ogee canopies, crocketed and cusped; each niche is flanked by small square turrets set cornerwise, having small ornamented buttresses of two sets off. In each of these niches stood a small statue; only one however now remains, which is the figure of a knight in armour of the period. It has unfortunately lost its head, but the camail of banded mail on the shoulders shews that it probably had a bascinet. The sculpture of this figure is so minute that every part of the armour may be distinctly recognised. A long flowing beard hangs over the camail of banded mail, and the shield of triangular heater form is slung behind the left shoulder, supported by the guige; he wears a close jupon buttoned down the front, a belt round the waist supporting a pouch on the left side, behind which is a short dagger, whilst on the right is a longer one or couteau, and the long sword reaching to the ground hangs on the left side. The legs are cased in plate, with a ridge down the shin. The effigy is that of a tall powerful man with a full and rather fat face, of any age from thirty upwards, and is extended at full length, his head resting on his heaume, and his feet on a bull, the hands being raised over the breast in the attitude of prayer. The head is covered with a bascinet pointed at the top, with camail of banded mail attached, and the face is seen through the aperture. The eyes are wide open, and on the upper lip are moustaches which extend over the cheek part of the hood; here also is seen the mode of attaching the camail to the bascinet, which is also enriched with an ornamental border. The figure is represented as wearing the hauberk of banded mail, the jupon or pourpoint with its scaloped edge, over which there is a surcoat closely buttoned down the front, but open at the side, up to the hips, where it seems to be bordered with fine fur or fringe. The arms are cased in plate, the epauliéres being of two overlapping plates, with roundels in front, as also at the elbow joints of the coudiéres, where the banded mail of the hauberk is seen. The hands are covered with gauntlets of plate. The chaussons are of studded work, and are riveted on to plain genouilliéres, these project much. The legs are cased in plate, and the greaves have a ridge down the front of the shin ; the sollerets are of plate, and the spurs have large rowels, and are fastened with buckles. Across the chest is the guige to which the shield is attached ; it is small, of triangular heater shape, and hangs behind the left arm. It appears to be plain, but from its close proximity to the pannelling by the side of the tomb, its surface cannot be seen. Around the hips is the rich knightly belt or baldrick, ornamented with precisely the same quatrefoils and four leaved flowers as appear on the last monument No. II, and to it is attached by the usual chain the dagger, which is of very considerable length and lies along the right side. The figure is also crossed by a slanting belt to support the sword, which lies on the left side beneath the shield. The total length of the dagger is twenty-eight inches, the blade being twenty-one ; the total length of the sword is four feet two inches, the blade being three feet six inches. The ornaments of the belt and the sword and dagger are precisely the same in both monuments, producing the impression that both were made at the same time and by the same artist. The length of the figure from the point of the bascinet to the bottom of the heel is six feet six inches ; and the entire length of the monument from the point of the head to the extremity of the slab is eight feet four inches. This figure has not escaped mutilation, for part of the right arm has been broken away and replaced with plaster, and the crest has also been broken from the heaume, so that we have here nothing heraldic to guide us.

Now the question arises as to whom this monument is intended to commemorate. Both Archdeacon Coxe and Mr. Daniel Rowland in his beautiful work "The History of the Neville Family," consider it the monument of Edward Neville, the first Lord of Abergavenny of that name, who married Elizabeth, daughter and sole heiress of Richard Beauchamp Lord of Abergavenny, and died 1476. This can however hardly be the case, as the armour of the figure indicates the date as the middle of the previous century, and this will be apparent at once to any one who compares it with the monuments of the XV century, which we shall soon have to consider. They have probably arrived at this erroneous conclusion by being misled by the bull at the feet of the figure, the bull being the crest of the Neville family, but the knight would hardly have had his crest at his feet. A bull's head was also the crest of the Hastings family, and it is quite possible that the bull may have had some heraldic signification, or have had relation to some circumstance connected with the family. Churchyard gives in his poem a traditional story of the knight having had an encounter with a bull; such a thing is very possible; he must however have been a bold as well as a powerful man to have taken the bull by the horns in the way described, and I must leave the readers to decide what amount of faith they will place in the story so related. Of this monument Symonds says,—" Another monument between the pillars of this chappel and the quire, not much unlike the former statue. Upon an altar tombe. A sword and long dagger. Not crosselegged. On his left arme a large shield, under his head a wyverne. A Neville say they," and accompanies it by a rough sketch of a helmet surmounted by the crest, a wivern. Churchyard also says,—" under his head a dragon ;" therefore there can be no error, but the crest is certainly perplexing, as it is neither the family crest of the Hastings or Neville, but of the latest of the Herberts. Crests were, however, arbitrary in many instances, and may have been assumed by an individual for some special reason, and, perhaps, not continued by his successor. The armour clearly points to the middle of the XIV century, and when we look at the succession of the Barons of Abergavenny, we shall find one, the date of whose death precisely coincides with the date of the armour, viz :—Lawrence de Hastings, who died 1348, aged thirty ; and we are moreover expressly informed that he was buried in the Priory Church at Abergavenny. His father died earlier in the century in 1325, and the armour will not suit that date, nor do we know if he was buried there. His son and successor died 1373, and was buried first at Hereford, and afterwards removed to the Grey Friars in London ; and his son, again, died 1389, and was also buried in the Church of the Grey Friars, so that there is no other Lord that it can be, and if it is not the monument of Lawrence, where is his monument ? The richness of armour and dress at once indicate that he was a personage of high consideration, so that I think we may fairly come to the conclusion that this is really the monument of Lawrence de Hastings, Lord of Abergavenny, who died 13th August, 1348, and was buried in the Priory Church.

This is the last of the Lords of Abergavenny who are recorded to have been buried here, for on the failure of the male line of Hastings, the Barony passed to other noble families, whose chief seats, residences, and estates were not at Abergavenny.

There is, however, one monument or effigy mentioned by Churchyard which is not easily identified, unless it be the wooden figure, of which he makes no special mention. He describes it as having been removed from the middle of the church, and placed in a window, but he does not say at what time. His words are " Amid the church Lord Hastings lay," and that " since his death his tombe had been removed away by fine device of man," and " layd within a windowe right full flat on stonie wall." Certainly the wooden effigy has reposed on the window sill for a very long time, and if he does not speak of that figure it is difficult to understand to what he alludes ; he does not say more of it than that "under his legges was a lion red." The feet of the wooden figure rest on a lion; he also speaks of the window above as filled with stained glass, and having portraits or figures of a lady and gentleman with armorial bearings. As the figure was moveable, it need not have had any connexion with the window, on the sill of which it was placed, or the coats of arms in it ; and the wooden figure may very well have been placed there in safety out of the way ; for being older than the church, it had no fixed resting place of its own, and was a loose and moveable object. The arms mentioned by Churchyard as being in the window, viz :—"the ragged sleeve" are those of Hastings, or, a maunch gules ; "and the sixe red birds" are clearly intended for those of de Valence, and these coats indicate John de Hastings the first of the name, who lived from 1272 to 1313, and probably built or contributed to the building of the New Church, and Isabella his wife, who was daughter of William de Valence, Earl of Pembroke, and sister and co-heiress of Aymer de Valence. The "Sixe white lyons the ground fayre blew," is the coat of Leybourne, and the "three flower-de-luces on ground of red hew" is that of Cantelupe. All these coats together pointed to John de Hastings, the second of that name, who married Juliana, daughter and heiress of Thomas de Leybourne. He seems to have assumed the de Valence arms, viz :—barry arg. and az. with an orle of six martlets gules, and borne them in the form of a bordure to his own, by placing his own Hastings coat, or, a maunch gu. on an escutcheon in the middle of the de Valence shield, the orle of birds serving for a bordure to it ; thus incorporating the devices of two distinct shields into one coat, viz, or, a maunch gules, within a border of Valence ; and as Mr. Boutel observes, is "a remarkable instance of the use of a bordure for the purpose of marshalling arms as a prelude to quartering." The coat of Valence was, however, peculiarly adapted for such an arrangement. The arms mentioned by Churchyard are thus all explained and identified, and being in a window, seem rather to have more reference to the structure of a church than to a monument, and to point to the builder of that portion of the church, the individuals who bore the arms, and the architecture of the church being contemporaneous.

But there is still a missing monument, which must have been destroyed before the time of Churchyard ; for he most distinctly states that upon the "tombe in stone" of this or some Lord Hastings " Were fourteene lords that knees did bow unto this lord alone ;" and then concludes

> "Of this rare worke a porch is made
> The barons there remaine,
> In good old stone and auncient trade
> To shew all ages plaine."

And in the margin is added, " Some say this great Lord was called Bruce and not Hastings, but most doe hold opinion he was called Hastings." The wooden effigy will not explain this, and would have formed no part of this tomb. This account can only refer to the early destruction of some altar tomb, the stone work of which had been used in the construction of a porch. Whatever may have been the date it is impossible to say, for all traces of both monument and porch have now vanished; but it may very probably have been the tomb of either the first or second John, Lord Hastings.

No. IV.

SIR WILLIAM AP THOMAS.

We now arrive at another series of knightly monuments of a different age, a different family, and a different material. The Barony of Abergavenny had by marriage passed into other families who were settled in distant parts of the country, where they held important ancestral Lordships, and as they ceased to live here, they ceased also to be buried in the Priory Church; and perhaps having been personally but little known in the locality, their ancestors seem to have been less thought of or cared for, and have in consequence been pushed into the cold shade of oblivion, from which I have endeavoured to rescue them, by another family, who were neither Lords of Abergavenny, nor indeed connected with the Lordship. These have taken their place in the church which the Lords of the XIII and XIV centuries had very probably built and adorned, and have given their name to this part of the structure, which is now called the Herbert Chapel; and it is very possible that the monumental tomb of Lord Hastings, which Churchyard informs us "laye amid the church," and had since his death been "removed away by fine device of man," was removed to make room for one of these monuments which now stand amid the church. These monuments were erected to different members of the Herbert family; they are of the XV century, and instead of being of freestone are constructed of alabaster.

This material is perhaps the most beautiful and best adapted for this kind of monumental sculpture of any that has been used. Its rich creamy and mellow tone of colour and waxy lustre contrast favourably with the hard, sharp, and cold whiteness of statuary marble, and its softness enables it to be easily worked with great delicacy and precision of detail. There is a paper upon this subject in Vol. X of the Archæological Journal, which gives much information. The most ancient remaining example of a finely sculptured effigy in alabaster is the cross-legged figure, said to represent Sir John Hanbury, in Hanbury Church, Staffordshire, of the date 1240. The material, however, does not seem to have been much employed till a century later; but from the middle of the XIV century it gradually came into general use, and so continued till the beginning of the XVII century. Its substance is a compact gypsum or sulphate of lime, and when burned forms plaster of Paris, and this quality may probably have caused the destruction in ruthless times of many examples, certainly of the fragments of statues. Its geological position is in the new red sandstone, and its chief deposit is in Derbyshire, where at Chellaston and Burton-upon-Trent it has been largely worked for sculpture and monumental purposes for many centuries. The "marbellers" in alabaster of Burton were early celebrated, and the execution or production of these sculptured monuments was a great trade of the district. Most of the finest medieval monumental sculptures were of this material, and so greatly was it prized, that Gough informs us that an alabaster monument for John, Duke of Bretagne, who died in 1399, was exported from this country to be erected in the Cathedral at Nantes, and that it was executed by three English workmen Thomas Colyn, Thomas Holewell, and Thomas Popplehouse, to whom King Henry IV granted a passport to carry it over in February, 1408. The monument, however, no longer exists. We may therefore infer that the making of these monuments was a peculiar English trade, and that the monuments were all executed at the quarries, and sent thence to their destination to be erected.

Here we have still to encounter the difficulty of identification, although the personages to whom they were raised were not only well known by their historical fame, but were also connected with families long resident in the country, so that in early times there never was any doubt respecting them; nevertheless Gough in his additions to the text of Camden, from a manuscript of the date of 1646, does throw some doubt on the first we are about to consider, especially on the lady, and this difficulty is strengthened by the information given us by Symonds, who visited the church the previous year. The first which comes chronologically under our notice is that of Sir William ap Thomas, illustrated by Nos. IV. and V. in the photographs. This is in the form of an altar tomb having on it two recumbent effigies of a knight and a lady, representing as has ever been believed, Sir William ap Thomas and his last wife, Gwladys, daughter of Sir David Gam. The tomb has been fearfully mutilated, if not altogether destroyed, for I have very great doubts whether anything which we now see, except the two recumbent figures formed any part of the original monument; and the best description of it would be a large block of rough masonry cased on the two sides and one end with slabs of sculptured alabaster, having on it two recumbent effigies of the same material. Through the raising of the pavement the lower part is altogether buried, and it also wants the upper slab with bevelled margin on which was usually the inscription; but as no inscription is mentioned in Churchyard, Symonds, or Gough, perhaps there never was one. The two sides are cased with sculptured slabs, there being four on each side, each two feet wide, but so put together that the south side of the tomb is eight feet seven inches long, and the north side nine feet long, one slab projecting six inches beyond the length of the tomb. Each of these slabs is divided into four shallow niches or compartments, on which stand on bracket pedestals small figures of saints and other holy persons, each holding a long upright scroll, on which however there are no legends. The backs of these niches, if not the figures themselves have been painted red, and most of the figures have at the back of the head a nimbus of blue, red, and gold. Over the heads of each of these figures is a small canopy, which projects but slightly, and has not a high triangular crocketed head as is usual, but one nearly horizontal, composed of small triangular pediments between small angular buttress-shaped pendants which form the angles, whereby the unfinished top of these canopies is exposed to view. The foot of the monument which is four feet wide, is similarly cased with three slabs in as many compartments, the centre being two feet wide, and representing the Annunciation of the Virgin under a wider canopy, of similar form to those at the sides; the two side compartments have each an Angel censing the Virgin. The three slabs were, however, rather too wide for the four foot space, and a portion of one has been cut off, apparently shewing that these sculptured slabs were not intended for the position they now occupy. The end of the tomb at the head is made up with a portion of a gravestone, an incised slab with a cross of very late date. These alabaster slabs, which are much broken and injured, reach from the pavement without moulding or ornament of any kind to the top of the tomb, on which are placed the slabs of the figures imbedded in common mortar. At the head of each effigy is placed a mutilated canopy; that over the lady being smaller than that over the knight. They are painted internally with red, blue, and yellow, exactly corresponding in style and design with those which form the sides of the tomb. The entire length of the tomb is nine feet, whilst the slabs with the figures are only six feet seven. None of these slabs have the least appearance of having been intended for a tomb, but on the contrary have much more the character of having been decorations for an altar. The church was as we know dedicated to the Blessed Virgin, and I have little doubt that what is now the chancel, where the communion table stands, was anciently the Lady Chapel, at the back of the high altar, which would have stood at the end of the choir in front of it, being probably parted from it by a screen, but having an entrance to it by doors on either side; and that the altar of the Lady Chapel was ornamented with a reredos of sculptured alabaster. This was of course removed at the Reformation, and when the monuments were destroyed by the Parliamentarian soldiers, the slabs and other remains of this reredos may probably have been used for their reparation. The canopies at the heads of the figures were never intended to be in their present position, for independent of their mutilation they were never wrought out or finished at the top, and all the rough work appears, and that is more conspicuous in the smaller canopy than in the larger. This idea seems to be confirmed by Symonds, who says nothing of the canopies, but speaks of angels and shields of arms behind the heads; and had they been there in the original state of the monument, it is strange that neither Churchyard, Symonds, or the author of Gough's manuscript should have made any mention of such striking and important portions of it. Now these eight slabs are just calculated to form a reredos of two tiers, four being in each tier, having in the centre of the lower the Annunciation, with the two Angels censing, and over that centre compartment the larger canopy, beneath which would stand the crucifix, whilst in the upper tier there might have been in the centre the coronation of the Virgin, now placed at the back of the recess among the children, over the monument of Sir Richard Herbert, of Ewyas, with whom or with whose children the coronation of the Virgin could have no special connexion ; whereas these two, the most important events in the history of the Virgin, would find their proper place in such a reredos, each being surmounted by a canopy. If this were the original arrangement of the church, it would exactly explain the purpose of a small single light window looking into the church from some apartment in the Priory, from which the high altar would be seen ; whereas, if it stood where the present communion table stands, it could not be so seen. It therefore seems to me probable that this monument was altogether destroyed, and that when it was repaired, a block of masonry was prepared of sufficient size to take four of these alabaster slabs on each side, and whereas the effigies were not sufficiently long to occupy the span on the top, the two canopies were placed there to fill up the vacancies ; besides, one being smaller than the other, they do not look as if they were intended to lie side by side, but might very well have been placed one above the other. This idea has been suggested to my mind, not merely by the patchwork condition of the tomb, but by the apparent age of the work. The date of the monument of Sir William ap Thomas must be as nearly as possible 1450, a very good period of art, whilst all this alabaster work, except the two effigies, has all the character of being the work of the end of the century.

We will now proceed to consider the effigies themselves, but we are met in limine by the description given of this monument in Symonds' Diary 1645, as also of 1646, quoted by Gough. Symonds describing this monument says, " In the middle of the chappel a stately faire altar tombe ; divers faire statues round about the sides. Upon the surface lyes two statues a man and woman, the man on the left hand. Under his head a helme, and forth of a wreath a maiden's head. A collar of S about his neck. At his head two angels support the shield." (A sketch is given shewing the arms of Herbert)" " Behind her head this." (Sketch of another shield giving arg : a lion rampant, sable crowned or.) " Bodies in alabaster. They call this forementioned monument Sir William Thomas, who was ancestor of the Herberts of Coldbrook, Ragland, and Werndee." The statement from Gough is as follows :—" Two altar monuments with the effigies in portraiture in alabaster in their armour. The first is Sir William ap Thomas, as there said, who married the daughter of Sir David Jones,"—(A mistake for Gam.)—" but I believe it is Thomas ap Gwillim Jenkin, father to Sir William Thomas, because that at the head of his wife that lies on his right hand in full portraiture, in an escocheon, is the black lion rampant crowned or, being the arms of Morley, who, as divers books being in my custody doth evident, the wife of

Thomas Gwillim ap Jenkin. She indeed was the daughter and heiress of Sir John Morley of Raglan, by whom the inheritance of Raglan and a great estate belonging to it first came to that family. Whether the daughter and heiress of Sir John Morley was wife to Thomas Gwillim Jenkin, or wife to Sir William Thomas, his son, it is by tradition diversely reported. The arms on this monument at the man's head is paly B : and G : three lions rampant or. The crest the Prior's head with a wreath above it." This seems to throw some doubt as to the monument being that of Sir William ap Thomas. Churchyard also mentions the same arms as being at the heads of both figures, at the time of his visit in 1586, except that he says that the Herbert lions are white. Therefore the fact of there being at that time an escocheon of arms "behind" the lady's head bearing a black lion rampant crowned or is confirmed, and is not easy to explain. These arms are the reputed coat of Sir John Morley, and if so, were not those of either of the wives of Sir William ap Thomas; and the tomb cannot be that of Thomas ap Gwilym Jenkin and Maud his wife, as Gough's M.S. supposes, for they are both recorded on the memorial stone in the church of Llansaintfraed, to have been buried there. This stone was set up in the chancel by William Jones, in 1624, to the memory of his ancestors, beginning with Thomas ap Gwilym Jenkin, who died 1438, and ending with Walter Jones, and Lettice his wife, his father and mother, who died in 1606 and 1623, giving the dates, and stating where they were buried. This effigy, moreover, could not have been that of Thomas ap Gwilym Jenkin, for he was not a knight, and could hardly have worn the collar of SS, even if he had been buried there, and he was not a person of such consequence as to have such a monument. Maud is styled *co-heiress* of Sir John Morley, but that strictly speaking she could not be, as Sir John had a son Gwilym, who was a father to a Philip. It must, however, be observed that the Welsh heralds generally styled those ladies heiresses who carried any landed property to their husbands, but she does not appear to have been so considered, as her arms were not quartered by the family.

How then came the arms of Morley at this lady's head? Of Sir John Morley, Mr. Wakeman writes as follows :—" Who Sir John Morley was, " whence he came, or who he married appears to be totally unknown. " Most probably he was some retainer of the Beauchamps, who were then " Lords of Abergavenny, and either by grant from them, or by marriage ob- " tained a little estate. The marriage of his daughter with Thomas ap " Gwilym is prominently put forward in all the pedigrees of the Herberts, " and not without reason, for Thomas ap Gwilym himself appears to have " been a person of unimportant condition. He is the first of the family of " whom we have any certain account, and the rise of the family must be " attributed to his son, Sir William ap Thomas." There is no doubt that at the time of the creation of the second Earl of Pembroke, in the reign of Edward VI., great exertions were made to raise his ancestors into high importance, and it is possible, though hardly probable, that in the XVI. century the monument, having been injured, or become shabby, may have been "restored," and the arms which passed for those of Morley have been painted on the shield at the head of the lady, either to record the match which was considered important, or in consequence of a belief which seems to have prevailed, that Sir William ap Thomas had married the daughter and co-heiress of Sir John Morley, and with her inherited large estates; but it is equally possible that that belief arose in consequence of the arms painted at the lady's head being wrongly attributed to Sir John Morley. There may be some ambiguity in the precise meaning of the words by which the position of this shield is described. Churchyard says that the shields stand "behind his head" and "behind her head." Gough's M.S. says the shield is "at the head of his wife," and in describing the next monument, which is in a similar style, he says, "her arms were in her escocheon at her head." Symonds says, "at his head two angels support the shield," and "behind her head is a shield." These words might apply to figures bearing shields on the body of the tomb, but nothing is said about the body of the tomb, and all the angels, shields, and arms are utterly destroyed; from these expressions I am inclined to infer that the angels and shields were on the top of the tomb close behind the heads of the effigies; and that the arms on the shield at her head were those which she bore; they therefore could hardly be the arms of Morley, with which family she had no connexion. Being the daughter of Sir David Gam, she would naturally have borne those of her father, though a widow. I am, however, not able to ascertain what arms he actually bore. He was entitled to bear the arms of Blethyn ap Maynarch, sa : a chevron between three spear heads arg : imbrued as also of Einion Sais, argent. three cocks gules, being lineally descended from them; but he may have gained or assumed a special coat for himself, which his daughter may have taken. Jones, in his history of Breconshire, give these arms as the coat of Rhys Grug, who was the son of Gryffydd ap Rhys, Prince of South Wales, and makes no mention of Morley; his daughter was the second wife of Einion Sais, and Sir David Gam may also have assumed the coat; at all events his daughter bore it, and it subsequently became a quartering in the shield of the second Earl of Pembroke. These arms were not borne by the first Earl of Pembroke, for in a M.S. in the British Museum (Add : M.S. 6298) where the arms of the Knights of the Garter of that period are carefully drawn, these arms do not appear in his coat. But in the coat of the Earl of Pembroke, the second creation in the time of Edward VI., 1549, in a shield of seven quarterings this crowned lion is found, following close on the arms which we know Sir David Gam was entitled to bear. They are in this order :—1. Herbert with a bordure bezanté (a substitution for the bendlet of illegitimacy);

2. Blethyn ap Maynarch; 3. Einion Sais; and then follows 4. Arg: a lion ramp: sa: crowned, or, the coat in question; and this is followed by 5. Cradock; 6. Horton; and 7. Cantelupe. To these quarterings the names are all given, and to this No. 4 is given the name "Asheley." Now no such name or family is known in the district, it therefore seems as if this coat was then a puzzle, and that the English herald who compiled the M.S. not being able to identify the coat with any arms which he knew, put the name of some English family. It seems to have perplexed many, and I must confess I am unable to give any satisfactory explanation of the matter, except by supposing that this was the coat which her father, Sir David Gam, himself bore, or that she arbitrarily assumed some coat which did not belong to her family, which may or may not have been the coat of Morley, but which may have acquired that name in consequence of later generations not knowing to whom to attribute it.

The length of the figure of the knight is six feet four inches from the heel to the top of the head, which is we see still cased in a bascinet, the face being uncovered, but instead of a camail there is a mentonière and gorget of plate, and round the bascinet is a wreath of some ornamental work, formed of cordate leaves, twisted with a band studded with pearls. The body is armed with a breast plate, having a slight ridge down the centre, and the arms are also cased in regular plate armour. The shoulders are protected by small fluted pauldrons, like epaulettes, and there is also a fluted fan-shaped plate at the elbow joint. The gauntlets are formed of overlapping plates, the fingers not being separate, and the plates do not extend to the ends of the fingers. The various parts of the armour were enriched by a hatched border, which was probably gilded. Round the neck is a collar of S.S., having a lozenge shaped jewel appended to it. Below the breast plate at the waist are six taces, or broad overlapping hoops, to the lowest of which are attached by straps and buckles three small tuiles three inches deep, the centre one having a small notch cut in it for the convenience of the saddle. The legs are altogether cased in plates, having the same hatched border; and at the knees are fluted fan-shaped plates similar to those at the arms. The sollerets are formed by a series of overlapping pointed plates; the toes are, however, broken away. The spurs were very long, with large rowels, the traces of which only remain. Round the hips is the broad knightly belt of leather or some such material, ornamented with square plates of leaves and single roses, large and small, probably of goldsmith's work; it was fastened with a buckle, and the end terminated in a rich pendant. The sword is broken away, and the dagger is on the right side. The head rests on the helm, being the helmet worn over the bascinet in battle and in tilting, on the top of which is the crest, so placed as to be looking close against the canopy, which seems to indicate that the canopy is not in its proper place. The crest is a very important and interesting matter, because it is very peculiar, and is very faithfully and minutely given, and therefore as it is the crest still borne by some members of the Herbert family, it should be carefully described, as it has not always been, especially by the author of Gough's M.S.. Who first assumed and handed down this crest I cannot say, but it seems to bear relation to the wars with the Saracens. It is commonly mentioned as a "Moor's head," and that would signify a man's head, which it is not. According to the late Sir Charles Young, garter, this Herbert crest is a Moorish women's head, affrontée, couped at the shoulders, with long hair sable, three rings pendant at the ears, or, a wreath or band about the head tied at the end by a button. This agrees with the monument in every particular but the wreath or band, which is here shewn more in the nature of a turban, confined by a band, having long flowing ends hanging down. There can be no doubt that this is the crest which Sir William ap Thomas used and wore, and he seems to have borne the old Herbert arms, per pale az. and gu. three lions rampant, or, as Churchyard and Gough describe them. The lions have since been changed to argent. The same crests were not always continued by the descendants, for we have here in this family and in these very monuments instances to the contrary, for Sir Wm. Herbert sometimes bore a wyvern, and Sir Richard Herbert a sheaf of arrows. The feet of the knight rest on a lion ; and if the engraving given in Coxe was correct, the monument was then in tolerably good condition, but since that time it must have been sadly defaced. The nose is broken away, and the entire surface disfigured by the handiwork of the school-boys in cutting out their initials on every part of it.

The effigy of the Lady Gwladis, for so we must consider her, is a good example of the costume of her time. The head is dressed in the high horned head gear, rising in two points or lobes, one on either side of the face to a considerable height above the head, the hair being confined and kept in its place by a fret or network having jewels at the points of intersection, the other parts being ornamented with bands of gold embroidery. A long veil hangs down behind; round the neck are two rows of chain with a cruciform locket. She wears a close fitting undergarment with tight sleeves ; over this is the usual sleeveless gown with large armholes, close fitting at the top, but getting fuller after it passes the hips, and descending to the feet which it covers. Over all she wears a mantle fastened across the breast with a double cord, which hangs down in front, terminating in a tassel ; at the feet are the figures of two small boys, who hold the ends of the mantle.

Sir William ap Thomas, who is believed to be buried beneath this monument was a distinguished personage, as well from his reputed personal valour, and the great possessions which he had in this district (for there was then no county) as from the circumstance of his being the ancestor of all the noble families of Herbert. He was a native of this part of the country and probably of Abergavenny, which has reason to be proud of him and his descendants. He must have been the author of his own fortune, as he was the fifth son of Thomas ap Gwilym ap Jenkin, called of Perthire, who, as we have seen, married Maud, daughter of Sir John Morley, and here his upward pedigree must stop as far as any authentic documentary proof is known to exist, although the Heralds carry it back to the time of Henry I. The late Mr. Wakeman, (as also the late Mr. H. M. Hawkins,) after the most careful and persevering researches by the examination of every accessible document relating to the subject has failed to trace it higher by any valid documentary evidence, and has left on record his confirmed opinion that "the Herbert family owes its rise and subsequent importance firstly to "Sir William ap Thomas, who was steward of the Lordships of Usk and "Caerleon, &c., under Richard, Duke of York, and secondly to his son, "Sir William Herbert, the first Earl of Pembroke. Being his steward, Sir "William was high in the confidence of Richard D. of York, and his son "Edward, afterwards Edward IV., and in that situation acquired exten- "sive estates in this part of the country, which were considerably "augmented by marriages. On his death he was succeeded in his office "of steward of Usk and Caerleon by his son William, afterwards created "Earl of Pembroke. Both father and son were no doubt men of first- "rate abilities, and the offices they held and the favour of the York "family afforded them opportunity of acquiring possessions and enriching "themselves and their relations." He also observes, "Previous to the "reigns of Henry VI. and Edward IV. none of the descendants of "Jenkin, who lived in the reign of Edward III. and Richard II. appear "in any authentic records as landed proprietors, and we have only the "statements of the Arwydd Feirdd or Welsh bardic heralds, the compilers "of pedigrees, that they were Lords of Werndee, near Abergavenny "and Perthire, near Monmouth. But the records prove that neither of "these places belonged to them at any time like so early a period as that "represented. Llanllowell and Beachley never belonged to them at all, "and the sons of Sir William ap Thomas were the first who were called "Herbert." Who this Jenkin, or John as he is sometimes called (for Jenkin and John are said to be in reality the same name) was, has been a matter of doubt; and Mr. Wakeman not having found any authentic documents to guide him, begins his pedigree with him, whom he calls Jenkin or John ap Adam, that being the reputed name of his father, and who Adam was has been the point of difficulty. All that he had been able to learn of Jenkin is that he was "magister serviens," master sergeant, whatever office that may have been, of the Lordship of Abergavenny, and had a small estate in Llanvapley. In a document signed by him as a witness, his name follows immediately after that of the steward, who was the Lord's deputy; the office may therefore may have been of some importance. After his signature follows that of the præpositus or bailiff, the chief authority of the town or borough.

Sir William ap Thomas married first Elizabeth, daughter of Sir James Bluett, of Raglan, and widow of Sir James Berkeley, by whom he had no issue, and who died 1420. He married secondly Gwladys, daughter of Sir David Gam, and widow of Sir Roger Vaughan, of Bredwardine, who fell with her father at the battle of Agincourt, in 1415. By some he is thought to have had an intermediate wife, Cary ddu of Troy. But Cary ddu is generally thought to have been his mistress, and not his wife, and the children by her are marked in most pedigrees as illegitimate, though in one by Hugh Thomas they are not so. It is strange that none of the genealogies say whose daughter she was, although she is invariably described as of Troy, as if it had been her estate; and soon after 1432 Sir William ap Thomas was Lord of Troy parva, but whether in right of Cary ddu or by purchase does not appear. It is, however, certain that Sir Thomas Herbert, her son by Sir William ap Thomas, held that manor, till he was attainted and his estates seized by the crown.

By his second wife Gwladys, he had Sir William Herbert the first created Earl of Pembroke of that family, Sir Richard Herbert of Coldbrook, and three daughters. He is commonly considered to have been at the battle of Agincourt, in 1415; and Edmondson in his Baronagium Genealogium p. 263 states that he was made knight banneret, 1415; but the authority for this statement does not appear. The third year of Henry V. was from March 21st, 1415, to March 20, 1416. In August, 1415, the King landed in France and there knighted divers gentlemen, whose names are not recorded. In October following he fought the battle of Agincourt, but no mention is made of knights or knights bannerets made there, except the three who were knighted on the field for saving his life. Sir Harris Nicolas, in his "History of the Battle of Agincourt," gives the name of every knight, man-at-arms, and esquire in the army, but does not name any William ap Thomas. Hence Edmondson's statement seems to be erroneous; and in confirmation of this, in the calendar of Inq : post mortem, for the 8th year of Henry V., 1420, occurs this entry :—" Elizabetha quæ fuit uxor Gulielmi app Thomas, "*armigeri*" (not equitis nor militis), nulla tenuit in com : Hereford, nec. "March ; Wall." This seems conclusive ; but furthermore, if he were knighted as Edmondson states in 1415, he was certainly knighted a second time by Henry VI. in 1426, which could not have occurred, for we find in Leland's Collectanea, Vol. II., p. 491, in a copy made "Oute "of a booke of Chroniques in Peter College Library," the following entry : "Henry VI scant XII months old began his reign, anno. 1422. In the "fourth year of his reigne (1426), Henry was made knight at Leycester, "by the Duke of Bedford, on Whit-Sunday, and after the King made "these knights," which knights are all mentioned by name, and among them is " Syr William ap Thomas." It is therefore quite clear that he was knighted by Henry VI. in 1426, and not by Henry V. in 1415 ; and that he did not then bear the name of Herbert.

As steward of the Lordship's marcher of Usk and Caerleon, which were small sovereignties, he was an important personage, being the lord's deputy, and the chief person in authority during the lord's absence. Besides this he was himself possessed of very large estates, being the owner of Raglan Castle. It must however be borne in mind that the Castle of Raglan was not at that time the magnificent structure which it afterwards became, and of which we now see the splendid ruins; but judging from the architecture, great additions seem to have been made in his time or that of his son the Earl; and, it is by no means improbable that the magnificent gatehouse, with its angular towers and bold machicolated parapets, may have been his work.

On the subject of his being owner of Raglan Castle and estate, Mr. Wakeman says "The often repeated assertion that the Herberts acquired
"the estate of Raglan, by the marriage of the father of Sir William ap
"Thomas with the heiress of a Sir John Morley, is totally erroneous. No
"such person as Sir John Morley ever possessed this manor, nor any
"other manor in the county that I can find." The descent of Raglan was as follows:—" The family of Bluet were Lords of Raglan through
"seven generations in the direct male line from Sir Walter Bluet the first
"subinfeudist under Strong-bow, in the reign of Henry II. John Bluet
"the seventh in descent from Sir Walter, left an only daughter Elizabeth,
"the wife of Bartholomew Pychard or Pycot, who in right of his wife had
"Raglan. Both were living in 1369, and had only one son John Pychard,
"who died without issue, and the estate descended to Elizabeth, the only
"daughter of Sir John Bluet, of Daglinworth in Gloucestershire, as
"second cousin and heir-at-law. This lady was then wife of Sir James
"Berkeley, to whom Henry IV. confirmed the manor by patent. Sir James
"Berkeley died in 1405, and his widow afterwards married Sir William ap
"Thomas, the ancestor of the Herberts. He did not however take Raglan
"in her right, but purchased it of her eldest son, James, Lord Berkeley,
"and the original conveyance deed is still among the muniments of the
"Duke of Beaufort, at Badminton."

Sir William ap Thomas died in 1446, and his wife, the Lady Gwladys, in 1454, which years give us the date of this monument. His will is not to be found, nor is there any inquisitio post mortem to shew what estates he possessed. As his first wife died in 1420, he could hardly have married Gwladys before 1422. Sir William Herbert, his eldest son, may therefore probably have been born about 1423 or 4. I have not found the date of his knighthood, which would be some guide. Immediately, however, on the accession of Edward IV, 4th March, 1461, he was summoned as Sir William Herbert to the King's first council, held March 10th. On the 4th November the same year, a parliament was held, at which Sir John Skidmore of Herefordshire and divers other persons were attainted, and their lands forfeited to the crown, and on that same day he was created Baron Herbert of Chepstow, Raglan, and

Gower ; and shortly after his creation he had a grant by patent of the Castle and Lordship of Pembroke, and several other manors in tail general among them the Lordship of Magor, Redwick, the Castle and Lordship of Caldicot in the Marches of Wales ; also the Castle of Goderich and Lordship of Urkenfield in Co : Hereford, late the estate of James, Earl of Wiltshire, attainted. Thus we see how persons in favour with the crown were enriched, and how they obtained such large possessions by the acquisition of the forfeited estates. In 1462 he was elected Knight of the Garter, and in 1463 he was appointed by patent Chief-justice of North Wales for life, and a grant of the Castle and Lordship of Dunster and Mynehede, late the possessions of James Lutterel, attainted. In 1468, 27th May, he was created Earl of Pembroke, and in 1469 he was at the battle of Banbury, where he was taken prisoner, together with his brother, and beheaded. As, however, this is a historical event of much interest, and especially concerns his brother Sir Richard Herbert, whose monument comes next in our series, I have subjoined the account of the circumstances attending the battle and execution, extracted from Hall's Chronicles where everything is minutely detailed.

His will, dated 27th July, 9 Edward IV., 1469, was duly proved, and taken from the copy given in the Testamenta Vetusta of Sir Harris Nicolas is as follows :—

In nomine Jesu.—Item : I to be buried in the Priory of Burgavenny, under charge between my fader's tomb and the chancell, and the cost that should have be at Tynterne to be set upon the chancell as my confessor, &c., shall say ; and you my wife and brother Thomas Herbert and wyfe that ye remember your promise to me to take the order of wydowhood, as ye may be the better master of your owne to perform my wylle, and to help my children as I love and trust you, &c. And that C. tonne of * * * * * be geven to the cloyster of Tynterne, &c. ; and XX $l.$ to the Greyfreres, where my body shall lyght, and that my body be sent for home in all haste secretly by Mr. Leisone and certain freres with him, &c. To Dr. Leisone X. marks a yere to sing for my soule during his life, &c. Item : to two prestes to be found to sing afore the Trinitie at Lanteliowe for my soule, and for all the soules slayn in the field for two yere, &c. Item : that my almshouse have as much livelode as shall suffice to finde six poure men and one to serve them. Wife pray for me, and take the said order that ye promised me, as ye had in my lyfe my hert and love. God have mercy upon me and save you and our children, and our Lady and all the saints in hevyn help me to salvation.— Amen. With my hand the 27th day of July.—William Pembroke.

His wife of whom he speaks so affectionately was Ann, daughter of Sir Walter Devereux, and his brother Thomas was his half-brother, Sir Thomas Herbert of Troy, son of his father, by Cary ddu. His wish to be buried at Burgavenny, although he so precisely fixes the spot, does not seem to have been attended to, for he seems to have been buried at Tyntern, and his brother occupies the spot he selected for himself. The will is however important in one particular, as it identifies the tomb we have been considering as that of his father Sir William ap Thomas, and not that of Gwilym Jenkin, as the author of Gough's M.S. was led to think from the Morley arms. An inquisition was held on his death, wherein are enumerated all his vast possessions in the counties of Hereford, Gloucester, and the marches of Wales, wherein are included Glamorganshire, Pembrokeshire, and Brecon, and the district which now forms the County of Monmouth.

Extract from Hall's Chronicle, (qto. p. 273), written, 1548, the 8th year of King Edward IV., 1469.

" When King Edward was by divers letters sent to him certified that the great army of the northern men were with all speed coming to London, therefore in great haste he sent to Wyllyam, Lord Herbert, whom within two years before he had created Earl of Pembroke, that he should without delay encounter the northern men with the extremity of all his power. The Earl of Pembroke, commonly called the Lord Herbert, was not a little joyous of the King's letters, partly to deserve the King's liberality, which of *a meane gentleman* had promoted him to the estate of an Earl, partly for the malice that he bore to the Earl of Warwick, being the sole obstacle (as he thought) why he obtained not the wardship of the Lord Bonvile's daughter and heir for his eldest son. Whereupon he, accompanied with his brother Sir Richard Herbert, a valiant knight, and above six or seven thousand Welshmen well furnished, marched forward to encounter with the northern men. And to assist and furnish him with archers was appointed Humfray, Lord of Stafford of Southwick, (named but not created) Earl of Devonshire, by the King, in hope that he valiantly would serve him in that journey, and with him he had eight hundred archers. When these two lords met at Cottishold, they made diligent enquiry to learn where the northern men were, and so by their explorators they were ascertained that they were passing toward Northampton; whereupon the Lord Stafford and Sir Richard Herbert, with two thousand well horsed Welshmen, said they would go, view, and see the demeanour of the northern men, and so under a woodside they covertly espied them pass forward, and suddenly set on the rereward, but the northern men with such agility so quickly turned about, that in a moment of an hour the Welshmen were clean discomfited and scattered, and many taken, and the remnant returned to the army with small gain.

King Edward, being nothing abashed of this small chance, sent good wordes to the Earl of Pembroke, animating and bidding him to be of a good courage, promising him not a lonely aid in a short time, but also he himself in person royal would follow him with all his puissance and power. The Yorkshire men being glad of this small victory were well cooled, and went no further southward, but took their way toward Warwick, looking for aid of the Earl, which was lately come from Calais, with the Duke of Clarence, his son-in-law, and was gathering and raising men to succour his friends and kinsfolk. The King likewise assembled people on every side to aid and assist the Earl of Pembroke and his company. But before or any part received comfort or succour from his friend or partaker, both armies met by chance in a fair plain, near a town called Hedgecote, three mile from Banbury, wherein be three hills, not in equal distance, nor yet in equal quantity, but lying in manner although not fully triangle. The Welshmen got first the west hill, hoping to have recovered the east hill, which if they had obtained, the victory had been theirs, as their unwise prophesies promised them before. The northern men encamped themselves on the south hill. The Earl of Pembroke and the Lord Stafford, of Southwick, were lodged at Banbury the day before the field, which was St. James's-day, and there the Earl of Pembroke put the Lord of Stafford out of an inn, wherein he delighted much to be for the love of a damsel that dwelt in the house, contrary to their mutual agreement by them taken, which was that whosoever obtained first a lodging should not be deceived nor removed. After many great words and crakes had between these two captains, the Lord Stafford of Southwick in great despite departed with his whole company and band of archers, leaving the Earl of Pembroke almost desolate in the town, which with all diligence to his post lying in the field unpurveyed of archers, abiding such fortune as God would send and provide. Sir Henry Neville, son to the Lord Latimer, took with him certain light horsemen, and skirmished with the Welshman in the evening, even before their camp, where he did divers valiant feats of arms, but a little too hardy he went so far forward that he was taken and yielded, and yet cruelly slain, which unmerciful act the Welshmen sore rued the next day or night, for the northern men being inflamed and not a little discontented with the death of this noble man, in the morning valiantly set on the Welshmen, and by force of archers caused them quickly to descend the hill into the valley, where both the hosts fought. The Earl of Pembroke behaved himself like a hardy knight and expert captain, but his brother Sir Richard Herbert so valiantly acquitted himself, that with his poleaxe in his hand (as his enemies did afterwards report) he twice by fine force passed through the battle of his adversaries, and without any mortal wound returned. If every one of his fellows and companions-in-arms had done but half the acts which he that day by his noble prowess achieved, the northern men had obtained neither safety nor victory.

Besides this behold the mutability of fortune. When the Welshmen were at the very point to have obtained the victory, the northern men being in a manner discomfited, John Clappam, Esq., servant to the Earl of Warwick, mounted up the side of the east hill, accompanied with only 500 men gathered of all the rascal at Northampton, and other villages about, having before them the standard of the Earl with the white, crying, "a Warwick, a Warwick!" The Welshmen thinking that the Earl of Warwick had come on them with all puissance, suddenly as men amazed they fled. The northern men pursued and slew without mercy, for the cruelty they had shewn to Lord Latimer's son ; so that of the Welshmen there were slain about 5000, besides them that were fled and taken.

The Earl of Pembroke, Sir Richard Herbert his brother, and divers gentlemen were taken and brought to Banbury to be beheaded. Much lamentation and no less entreaty was made to save the life of Sir Richard Herbert, both for his goodly personage, which excelled all men there, and also for the noble chivalry that he had shewed in the field the day of the battle, in so much that his brother the Earl when he should lay down his head on the block to suffer, said to Sir John Conyers and Clappam, "Masters, let me die for I am old, but save my brother which "is young, lusty, and hardy, mete and apt to serve the greatest Prince "in Christendom. But Sir John Conyers and Clappam, remembering "the death of the young knight, Sir Henry Neville, cousin to the Earl "of Warwick, could not hear on that side, but caused the Earl and his "brother, with divers other gentlemen to the number of ten to be "beheaded."

There is a remarkable expression in the early part of this narrative, where it is said that the Earl of Pembroke had been promoted from *a meane gentleman* to the estate of an Earl ; this certainly does not look as if he was considered to be descended from an ancient and distinguished line of ancestors.

No. V.

SIR RICHARD HERBERT, OF COLDBROOK.

Our next monument in chronological succession is the tomb beneath which Sir Richard Herbert, of Coldbrook, and his wife, Margaret, are believed to rest, and which is represented in Photographs VI and VII. This, like the last, is an altar-tomb of alabaster, once very rich and beautiful, but alas! it has undergone disfigurement, mutilation, and destruction equally with the last described. It stands under the arch, between the chapel and the choir, the head being very close to the pier of the arch, and occupies the precise spot designed by the Earl of Pembroke for himself; the body of the tomb is eight feet five inches long, and three feet nine inches wide; the base is buried, but the height of the tomb above the pavement is two feet nine inches; the north side consists of an arcade or series of nine shallow niches, with the backs flat and not recessed, surmounted with crocketed ogee canopies, and separated from each other by small buttresses terminating in pinnacles. This side is composed of four slabs, two containing three niches each, one of two niches, and one, the last, at the foot of the tomb consisting of a single niche, having no buttress at the angle. This will all be well seen in Photograph VII. In eight of these niches, standing on bracket pedestals, are angels or winged figures clothed in long robes, and having on their heads crowns, with a fleur-de-lis in the front, and a cross on the summit of an arch which spans the head from side to side, their hair being parted and spread out at the sides, forming as it were a brim to the crown. They all bear in front of them large shields. In the ninth and last at the head of the tomb, the figure is that of a man in armour, who bears before his breast a large shield similar to the rest. The whole is surmounted with an embattled cap moulding. The south side of the tomb is a mass of patchwork, as will appear in Photograph VI; at the head is a slab of three niches, similar to those on the north side; the figures are, however, two men in armour, with their hair parted, and spread out wide at the sides, the third figure being an angel; all three bear shields; then comes a slab of greater width, the centre of which contains a seated female figure holding a child in her right arm, apparently intended for the Virgin. In the niche on her right is a standing female figure, holding in her right hand before her body a sword pointing downwards; her left hand and some other object is broken away, but it was probably a portion of a wheel, and the figure is most likely that of St. Catharine: there seems to have been something at her feet, but it is too much broken to determine what it was. In the other niche is a female figure standing on a dragon, into whose mouth she is thrusting the end of a long staff, the top of which probably terminated in a cross, now broken off, but the small supports of the alabaster which sustained it still remain : this figure would, therefore, represent St. Margaret, very probably the patron saint of the Lady who bore her name. These three figures are each crowned with a coronet of ornamental trefoils or strawberry leaves as they are heraldically termed. Then follows a small narrow niche without figure, and the remaining portion is made up of fragmentary odds and ends of similar niches. Both ends of the tomb are blank ; that at the feet being composed of part of a flat grave-stone, whilst at the head it is seen that the alabaster casing extends six inches beyond the rough block of masonry, of which the body of the tomb is composed, and does not form part of it, being only attached by occasional iron cramps. These slabs of alabaster most probably formed part of the original tomb, which seems to have been quite destroyed, and the fragments refitted as far as could be, in the best manner their state would allow. The slab with the three Saints in all likelihood was at the foot of the monument, having the Holy Virgin in the middle, and the Patron Saints of the Knight and his Lady on either side, each below the proper effigy.

The two statues have both suffered much injury, the Knight more than the Lady. At the head of each is a sadly mutilated alabaster canopy, but that these belonged originally to the monuments may be doubtful, for no mention of them is made in any of the early accounts, and we are told in some that at the heads of each figure were escocheons with their arms. Symonds speaking of this monument says "the shields "are supported by angels round about the sides," also, "at his head not "impaled at all;" giving a sketch of the Herbert arms, "This at her "head;" and gives another sketch of a chevron between three eagles heads, sa: the birds are properly ravens, which he has mistaken for eagles heads. "He is in long black hair, under his head a helmet sur- "mounted by the crest, on a wreath, a bundle of arrows or,"—again from Goughs M.S. we learn that "her arms were in her escocheon at her "head, three ravens proper, sa:," therefore as the shields of arms were at the heads of the figures, it would be difficult to place the large canopies.

The effigy of the Knight is much injured, the right arm is broken away from the shoulder to the wrist ; it seems, however, to have been repaired at some time, as the dowel holes remain. The figure, from the crown of the head to the bottom of the heel, is six feet four inches, and represents a very tall spare and bony man. The head rests on the helm, which is surmonted by his crest on a wreath, a sheaf of arrows the points downwards ; and the lambrequin or mantling of the helm, lying on each side of the figure, forms a scaloped bordering drapery which terminates in the tassel ; this, however, on the outer side of the tomb has been broken away. It will be seen that he did not adopt his father's crest. He his bare-headed, having no bascinet ; the hair is cut short and square across the forehead, and is curled up at the points, and spread out at the sides of the head, and there is neither beard, whiskers, nor moustaches. The face is thin and looks older than his age (which could not possibly have been above 45, and was probably much below) would warrant. The throat is bare, and the under-garment which would be equivalent to the gambeson appears above the upper portion of the body armour. This consisted of an articulated cuirass or breast plate, formed for greater facility of motion of an upper and a lower plate, the lower part from the waist upwards rising in a point, and being fastened on the breast of the upper plate by a strap and buckle, which is clearly shown. The lower part of the cuirass is very small round the waist, below which it spreads out, and terminates in seven scaloped overlapping tassets, which are fastened together at the sides by small straps. To the fourth of these over each thigh are fastened also by straps and buckles the tuiles, which are scaloped and fluted. There are also tuiles behind, which are attached by similar means to those in front. Below the tassets, both in front and at the sides between the tuiles is still seen the skirt of chain-mail. The vambraces and rerebraces (the plates covering the front and back of the arms) were also joined with straps and buckles. The pauldrons were very large and heavy, and were attached to the cuirass in front with turn buttons, the upper parts of them standing up like a high collar. Round his neck he wears a chain or collar composed of alternate single roses and suns, two of the badges of the house of York, and to this is appended, as a jewel, a lion sejant. The gauntlets have cuffs, and are formed of overlapping round-topped plates, the ends of the fingers being bare. The plate armour, covering the legs and thighs, is fastened like the other parts with straps and buckles, and the genouillerés have two overlapping plates above, and two below the knees, and are buckled round the leg. The sollerets are also formed of articulated plates, which lap over upwards towards the knee; the feet rest on a lion, but the toes and spurs have been broken away; and, indeed, the legs have been broken and repaired, and, together with the lion, have evidently been exposed to the weather for a long period, as the stone is much weather worn and washed away from long exposure to the action of water. The whole figure is very spare, and the legs and thighs are remarkably slender for so tall and powerful a man as he is recorded to have been. The sword lay on the left side, but is broken away, it was attached to a narrow oblique cross belt, fastened with buckles in front. On the right side are the remains of a small dagger which was fastened to the armour by an oval link, and lay underneath the figure. Coxe has given an engraving of the upper half of this figure, taken on the left side. The features are made to look too old, and the helm supporting the head is omitted; the scaloped edges of the lambrequin are made to look like leaves, the draughtsman not knowing what they were.

We now come to the consideration of the Lady Margaret his wife; and if this effigy is a correct representation of her in point of size, she must have been of colossal stature and prodigious power, for the statue is of the same length as that of her husband, viz. : 6 feet 4 inches, and her whole figure is stout in due proportion. She has a full and perhaps handsome face ; but her nose, as well as that of her husband, is broken quite away, and the features are otherwise disfigured by the schoolboys' initials which have been cut upon them, as well as on every other smooth part of both statues. The head rests upon a cushion, which has a tassel at the back and at each side, and is supported by small figures of angels rising from little brackets. The hair is parted in the middle, and flows down on each side of the head, around which she wears an orle or wreath, in form similar to that round the helmet of Sir William ap Thomas ; it appears to be made of some material covered with a fret or network of gold, having what appear to be jewels, or some enrichment, at the points of intersection, and at intervals round the head are single roses probably of white enamel, being one of the Yorkist badges. Attached to it in front, and lying on the forehead, is a semicircular ornament, having in the centre a large square pointed diamond, with a row of other flat-topped stones, probably table diamonds, set round it. It may be well to observe here, that at that time the art of cutting diamonds was not known ; there were, therefore, neither rose-cut nor brilliant-cut diamonds, those which were worn being either flat-topped table stones, or the pyrimidal pointed diamonds, which were the natural octohedral crystal of the stone, and this form is indicated in the ornament in question. Round her throat she wears a rich carcanet, from which hang a row of pear-shaped drops, probably pearls, alternating with small crosses. Her dress, as far as we can see, consists of a close-fitting gown or juste au corps, coming up to the neck, and having tight-sleeves, ending in cuffs at the wrists ; over this is the sleeveless gown or kirtle with very large arm holes, through which we see a narrow strap or girdle, fastened with a buckle, passing obliquely across the body underneath it, the use of which is not apparent, but it may possibly have sustained a gypcière or purse. The kirtle becomes full at the skirt below the hips, and flows down, covering all the feet except the toes, which are broken off. Over all she wears a mantle, fastened across the chest with a double cord, which is attached to two ornaments at the edge of the mantle, in form of single roses ; this, after lying in loops upon the chest, passes through a fretted slide, and hanging down in front, ended in two tassels, which are broken off. The feet rest on two little dogs, wearing collars with bells on them, and they hold the corners of the mantle in their mouths. The hands, which are joined in the attitude of prayer, have rings on each finger, but each on a different joint, so that they may not come in contact with each other ; the little fingers have been broken away. The rings seem to have consisted of flat, fluted, or plain hoops of gold, set with single stones. The detail of this costume is most carefully and elaborately given, and it is a fine specimen of such artistic work.

I find the effigies of this monument are figured in an engraving in Sir Richard Colt Hoare's "History of Wiltshire," Vol. III., p. 140, where he is treating of Wilton and the family of the Earl of Pembroke. By some strange mistake they are given as the monument of Sir Richard Herbert, of Ewyas, ancestor of the Earls of Pembroke, being really the effigies of Sir Richard Herbert, of Coldbrook, and his wife, who had nothing to do with the Earls of Pembroke. In the plate they are accompanied with shields of the arms of Herbert, without the bendlet, which is most conspicuous in the real tomb of Sir R. Herbert, of Ewyas, and also the arms of Cradock, thus mixing up the two monuments by giving the figures of one with the arms of the other; and in the lettering it is styled the monument of Sir R. Herbert, of Ewyas. It is a very remarkable circumstance that so able a man as Sir Richard Hoare, who had visited Monmouthshire in company with Archdeacon Coxe, and made many of the drawings for his tour of the county, should have made so great a mistake, and fallen into such an error, for on the Ewyas monument that word is most distinct, that being, in fact, the only monument of the series which has any inscription. This is an instance how serious errors sometimes find their way into works of great weight and authority, and having once so appeared are perpetuated by subsequent writers copying what they see in print, without taking the pains, or perhaps not having the means, of verifying the statements. I do not know whether this error has ever been discovered or noted before; probably not, for the Abergavenny monuments have hitherto been little known or cared for.

Sir Richard Herbert, of Coldbrook, was second son of Sir William ap Thomas and his wife, Gwladys, daughter of Sir David Gam; he was therefore, as we have seen, younger brother to the Earl of Pembroke. Of the date of his birth we have no knowledge, but it could not possibly have been before 1425, and most probably did not occur till many years after, for his brother, the Earl, at the time of his death when he could not have been above 45, describes himself as old, and calls his brother young; there must therefore most likely have been a considerable disparity of years between them. He married Margaret, daughter of Thomas ap Gryffydd, and sister to the renowned Sir Rhys ap Thomas, so celebrated in the placing Henry VII on the throne. When he was knighted does not appear; but Lewis Dwn, in his "Visitations of Wales," p. 312, calls him a "Knight of War, and of the Coronation," leaving it to be inferred that he was knighted at the coronation of Edward IV. This, however, is certainly not correct, for there exists a most important document which proves the contrary. The accession of Edward IV. was on the 4th March, 1461, his coronation took place on the 29th June that year, a most important Parliament was held on the 4th November following, and in a document, which is dated the 20th February following (1462), he is styled Richardus Herbert Armiger. Two things are quite clear from this document first, that he was not then a knight; and secondly, that at that date, although his father was only Sir William ap Thomas, he and of course his brother, then Sir William, had assumed the name of Herbert as their permanent surname. This document is one of very great importance in the history of Sir Richard Herbert, and seems to shew how persons and families of small estate and importance were enriched and elevated in the social scale; and we have seen how this family was enriched from its comparatively inconsiderable origin to be one of the wealthiest and most powerful in the realm. Thomas Gwilym Jenkyn, father of Sir William ap Thomas, was not in any way distinguished by position or wealth; and Sir William was the first who laid the foundation of the family by becoming steward of the Lordship's marchers in this part of the country to Richard, Duke of York, and thus, being a man of much ability, gained the confidence of his patron, and consequently got into favour with Edward IV.; his sons also gained the King's favour, and by their zealous services acquired considerable estates as well as high distinguished and well deserved dignities. This document is found among the Patent Rolls of the 1st Edward IV., and bears date 20th February, and the accession of the King being the 4th March, 1461, the first year extends to the same day, 1462; and it must have been in that year as that was the first February in his reign.

My kind friend Mr. Burtt, of the Record Office, has been so obliging as to give me a copy of this curious patent, and I will give the principal portions of a literal translation :

"For Richard Herbert.—The King to all whom, &c. Health.—Know
" that we of our special grace, and for good and laudable service which
" our beloved servant Ricardus Herbert, armiger, hath rendered to
" us before this time, have granted, and for our heirs by these presents do
" grant to him the manor and Lordship of Mockas, and the manor of
" Grove with its appurtenances in the County of Hereford, and all the
" lands, tenements, possessions, and hereditaments, which were of late
" the property of John Skidmore, knight, in the aforesaid county, and
" in the counties of Gloucester and Salop, as also in Wales and the
" marches of Wales, which manors, Lordships, land, and tenements and
" other premises by reason of the forfeitures of the same John, and of a
" certain act passed in our Parliament at Westminster, on the 4th day
" of November last passed, came into our hands as they ought to come."
" We moreover granted to the same Richard Herbert the manor of
" Mounton, the manor of Feú, and the moiety of the manor of Eton,
" near Rosse, in the said county, and other lands and possessions which
" were the property of Thomas Fitzharry, late of Hereford, Esquire,
" which by reason of his forfeiture have come into our hands, to be held
" by the said Richard Herbert and his heirs in tail male, at the value of
" £100 of us and our heirs, &c. Teste Rege apud Westmonasteriam,

"XX die Februarii. By writ of privy seal of same date." This shews how these things were done, and it is possible that many estates were so given without the formality of a patent.

The attainder of Sir John Scudamore was, however, reversed in 1472-3, saving of letters patent in favour of William Herbert, son and heir of Sir Richard Herbert, Knight, except as to grants to Richard Herbert of the lands of Sir John Scudamore. It is therefore evident from this document that he had been early a staunch adherent and faithful servant of the Yorkist cause. He appears to have been a man of fine personal appearance, great stature, and physical strength and power, though I think we should hardly infer from the features any unusual personal beauty.

How or when the family acquired Coldbrook does not appear, but he is not described in that document as of Coldbrook. It is possible that he may have received it from his father, who had large possessions in these parts; all that is known for certain is that Sir Richard was settled there as his chief residence, though he also resided in the Castle of Montgomery, of which he either had a grant, or held it in virtue of some office. As part of the present mansion of Coldbrook is of great antiquity, it is very probable that he may have built the first dwelling house, which has with the advance of time necessarily received considerable additions, and undergone great alterations at various later periods.

His eldest son, Sir William Herbert, succeeded him in that estate, and continued to reside at Coldbrook. His second son, Sir Richard, was steward of the Lordships and marches of North Wales, and resided at Montgomery Castle, and from him was lineally descended Lord Herbert of Cherbury, who married Mary, daughter and heiress of Sir William Herbert of St. Julians, where he came to reside. Lord Herbert of Cherbury, in the introduction to his own autobiography, describes the wonderful and gallant prowess of the Earl of Pembroke and Sir Richard Herbert of Coldbrook at the field of Banbury.

No. VI.

SIR RICHARD HERBERT, OF EWYAS.

We now come to the last of the Herbert Monuments, that of Sir Richard Herbert, of Ewyas, as he is called, which is represented in photograph VIII. This is also of alabaster and occupies a recess in the south wall of the Herbert chapel, flanked by two buttresses set cornerwise, and capped with crocketed pinnacles. Over the recess is a crocketed ogee canopy, and the face of the wall above the recess between the buttresses terminates in an embattled cap moulding, above which rise the pinnacles of the buttresses at the ends, and the finial of the canopy in the centre. This monument has fortunately not suffered quite such destructive mutilation, though it has probably been disturbed from its original position, as all the stones appear to have been removed and reset in their former places. The basement, as will be seen by the photograph, is below the present pavement, and that portion of the bed of the monument which is above it, exhibits a row of nine niches or panels, capped each with two small crocketed canopies, having a small angular buttress shaped pendant between them, the centre niche being wider than the others. The group or whatever else may have been there has been removed, and the piece of carved stone which now stands there does not belong to it, having been placed there not many years ago, and was certainly not there when Mr. Blore made his beautiful drawing of the monument. It seems to have been portion of a spandrel of some other structure, and contains a figure of an angel kneeling; to what it belonged cannot now be determined, but there is a fragment exactly similar fixed up against the side of the tomb of Andrew Powell. The other eight niches are occupied by as many seated figures, two of which on each side bear shields before their breasts; the remainder seem to be persons in ecclesiastical garb, two of them holding open books in their hands. Above this is the slab on which the effigy lies, on the sloping verge of which is sculptured in raised black letter characters the monumental inscription, which by the aid of a magnifying glass may be clearly read in the photograph, and it is the only inscription we meet with in the whole series of tombs, to indicate whom they belong; it is now as follows: "Hic jacet Richardus Herbert de Ewyas miles qui obiit nono die **** anno regni regis Henrici Octavi 2° cujus aia propitietur Jes.—Amen." There is, however, some mystery about this inscription, for only the latter half is original. It was of course first carved in the alabaster from end to end of the tomb, but unfortunately only the latter portion of the original alabaster inscription beginning with the words "Regni Regis" now remains. This will be clearly perceived in the photograph. All the former part has at some time been broken away, and replaced by an inscription cut in rough stone, in a style to correspond with the latter part, and that not in one continuous length, but seems to be formed with various fragments patched together with common mortar. Churchyard makes no mention of the inscription, but both Symonds and the author of Gough's M.S. saw the tomb in its original state, and both independently of each other copied the inscription, and here we fortunately have their respective versions of it. Symonds says "upon the verge this inscription guilt fairely"—"Hic jacet Richardus Herbert, armiger, qui "obiit XII die Septemb. a D'ni MCCCCCX.° a° Regni Regis Henrici " Octavi 2° cujus a' i' e p. d. a." Gough's author renders it, " Hic jacet " Richardus Herbert ar. qui obiit ij die Septemb. anno Dom, 1520, et " anno R. R. H. VIII. II." The date 1520 is clearly a clerical error, as the second year of H. VIII. was 1510. Thus we see that these two independent authorities concur in every important particular, that the words "miles" and Ewyas have been gratuitous interpolations in the inscription for some unexplained reason, probably at the time of the reparation of the monument ; and lastly, that he was simply an esquire and not a knight as we shall soon see further proved by incontestible contemporaneous documentary evidence. Churchyard also calls him a Squire three times.

The effigy measures six feet six inches from the heel to the crown of the head, which rests on a helm from which the crest is broken away, but Gough informs us it was a green dragon, that is a wyvern, the crest borne by the Earls of Pembroke. The figure is bare headed, the hair is cut short and straight across the forehead, and falling down on each side of the face, is also cut straight at the bottom. The cuirass which is now a single breast plate comes up to the throat, shewing the under garment in puckered folds above it ; it has a slight angular projection or ridge down the centre, and on the right side is shewn the contrivance for fixing the lance rest. The pauldrons are large and cut square at the arms, the upper part at the neck rising like a high stand up collar. He wears a large collar of SS, having as a pendant a large cross patée, of which the lower limb is the longest. The arms are cased in plate, and the coudiéres or elbow pieces are of large size and fantastic shape. The hands are bare and raised upon the breast in prayer, the gauntlets formed of large overlapping plates lying beside the figure. Round the small of the waist is a cord, below which the armour spreads out over the hips, and there are seen three tassets, to which are attached by straps large fluted tuiles, fourteen inches long, which meet in front, and are turned back at the edges, as if to give the appearance of being made of some flexible material. Below the tuiles is seen a skirt of chain mail, reaching nearly to the knee. The thighs as well as the legs are cased in plate, and the genouilliéres having at the sides ornamental plates are simple, without any overlapping plates above or below the knees, such as we have seen. The sollerets instead of being pointed and flat to the foot as heretofore, are very broad and high at the toes. The sword is broken away, but it lay on the left side, and was suspended by a narrow belt, which passes obliquely across the figure and is fastened with a buckle, the end being folded over in a knot, and terminating in an ornamented pendant. In the triangular space or spandrel between the low arch of the recess, and the ogee canopy above it, is a large scaloped shield of good form, bearing the arms of Sir Richard, viz : the later arms of Herbert, pr. pale az. and gules, three lions rampant argent, debruised with a bendlet or baton argent, as a mark of illegitimacy, impaled with the arms of Cradock, being those of his wife, azure, semèe of cross crosslets, three boar's heads couped argent. At the back of the recess is a singular group sculptured in alabaster. In the centre is a tall female figure in the costume of a lady of the time, wearing a close fitting gown, and over it a mantle fastened across the chest with a cord, the ends of which hang down. On her head she wears a veil which falls down behind. Her arms are broken off, but there is no appearance of her having held a child in them. Her feet are supported by an angel, and at her right side kneels a man in armour, and at her left a lady; above these on either side are two angels, one above the other as if supporting her. There is neither nimbus nor glory apparent about the head, but above it there seems to be an object like a triple crown held by a figure above, whilst on either side of it above her shoulders are two larger figures having very large glories or nimbi behind their heads, which are however broken off. On either side of the main figure are groups consisting of three small figures of men in armour, kneeling, having their helmets below them, and one female figure also kneeling; beneath each figure is a shield bearing the arms of Herbert and Cradock alternately. On the Herbert shield is the bendlet and also a small cresent in chief for a difference or mark of cadency. Beneath this row of figures is an embattled cap moulding partly coloured, which hardly seems in its proper place. The whole has evidently been taken down from some other place, for it does not fit its present position, and having been greatly injured has been clumsily refitted ; it is very dark and discoloured, and being at the back of the recess, and close under the soffit, it is not easy to discern clearly what is there. Some have thought that the chief figure represented his wife, the idea probably arising from her costume. But he and his wife with their eight children are there in adoration of the central figure ; and it seems to me that the group can only represent the crowning of the Virgin, and so Symonds who saw them uninjured describes it, and gives a rude sketch of it as it then was; in this it is quite clear that the object over the Virgin's head is a triple crown, which has been greatly injured, and that the three figures represent the three persons of the Holy Trinity who are jointly placing the crown on her head. Each figure himself wears a crown, and the right hands are raised in the act of benediction : the centre figure represents the Father having on his right hand the Son, who bore a cross, the stem of which may still be seen, and on his left the Holy Spirit. As the Son was represented in the Trinity there could be no infant in the arms of the Virgin. This central portion of the group is just 3 feet high, and what remains of it is so close to the soffit of the arch, that there could hardly have been space for the upper figure when entire, and certainly not for any border or margin. It is therefore evident to me that this was not its original position. These slabs have all been embedded in mortar, which is brought up level with their surface.

Sir Richard Herbert, of Ewyas, (for we must I suppose still continue so to call him, although his Knighthood seems to be a myth, not having been originally recorded on his tomb, and not found there till after 1647, and Ewyas seems to have been also an invention after that date) was a natural son of Sir William Herbert, Kt., the first Earl of Pembroke, by his concubine Maude, said to be the daughter and heiress of Howell Gwyn or Graunt, as the name is sometimes given, but which is uncertain as there is no known authority. Where she came from I know not, nor did Mr. Wakeman succeed in discovering. Whether he was of Ewyas may even now be doubted, for I have never been able to discover the reason why he was especially described as Sir Richard Herbert, of Ewyas, except from the name being found on his tomb. There were two very ancient Lordships Marcher of that name, Ewyas Lacy, and Ewyas Harold. The name Ewyas is of great antiquity, and existed before the Norman conquest, and its origin, derivation and meaning have never been satisfactorily explained. Ewyas Lacy very soon after the conquest was granted to William Fitz Osberne, and so became a border or Marcher Lordship. He was succeeded in possession by Walter de Lacy who gave his name to it, which it has ever since retained, and his son Roger held it at the time of the Domesday survey. In the latter part of the XV century, it was in possession of the Lords of Abergavenny, and has so continued. It was of considerable extent, and in the 27th of Henry VIII. A. D. 1531, was annexed to the County of Hereford as a separate Hundred, and occupies the south west corner of the County, being bounded by the Counties of Monmouth and Brecon, and is within a few miles of Abergavenny. Ewyas Harold (from whom its name is derived is not certainly known) was a Lordship of less extent, and was by the same act added to the hundred of Webtree, and was also at the same period in possession of the Lords of Abergavenny. He therefore has no connexion with the Lordships, and as an illegitimate son he could not have inherited any estate from his father, though it is quite possible that out of his vast possessions his father may have given him an estate, or he may have held or acquired some estate there on which he resided, and thus have obtained that description, I have not found any Inquisition to give the information, nor any will. Collins in his peerage states that he had a seat at Grove Radnor, but no one seems to know exactly where that is; and as Sir Richard Herbert, of Coldbrook, certainly had a grant of a Manor of Grove, it is very probable that some confusion may have been made between the two Knights.

He married Margaret, daughter and heiress of Sir Matthew Cradock, of Swansea, knight, and widow of John Malefant, of St. George's, and her arms appear impaled with his on the shield above the monument. By her he had two sons, Sir William Herbert, knight, the eldest, who was created Earl of Pembroke in 1551, from whom descend the Earls of Pembroke and Carnarvon, and the Marquis of Bute. His second son was Sir George Herbert, of Swansea, knight, who married Elizabeth, daughter and co-heiress of Sir Thomas Berkeley, of Vine, Co. Southampton, by Elizabeth Nevill, daughter of George Nevill, second Lord Abergavenny of that family. This Sir Thomas Berkeley bore the coat of Berkeley within a bordure, and his daughter, though not an heiress, quartered the Nevill coat of arms with that of Berkeley to mark her descent. Sir George Herbert died 1570. Symonds in his notes on this monument says, "these coats upon it," and then gives a rough sketch of a shield clearly intended for Herbert, impaling Berkeley and Nevill quarterly, which two coats are most clearly given, supported on one side by a man in armour, and on the other by a woman, with a mermaid for a crest. This can be no other than the shield of Sir George Herbert, impaling his wife's arms. The shield is now lost, but there can be no doubt that with its supporters it originally occupied the now vacant space in the middle of the front the of tomb, and would seem to indicate that he, Sir George Herbert, of Swansea, erected this monument to the memory of his father. In the catalogue of state papers of the time of Henry VIII. we find notice of the following writs of Privy seal extant in the Public Record Office which concern Richard Herbert:

1st.—An appointment for Richard Herbert, gentleman usher to Henry VII. to be Constable and Porter of Bergavenny Castle, dated Greenwich, 22nd July. 1. Henry VIII. (1509).

2nd.—For Richard Herbert to be receiver during pleasure of Bergavenny, in Marches of Wales, as formerly—dated Croydon, 12th April. 1. Henry VIII. (1510).

3rd.—For Charles Somerset, Lord Herbert, Chamberlain, to be Constable and Porter of the Castle of Bergavenny, and receiver of the said Lordship, in the King's gift by the decease of Richard Herbert—Also grant for 20 years of the farm of the demesnes and lands in the said Lordship at the rent paid by the said Richard dated 23rd September, 2. Henry VIII. (1510.)

The King held the Lordship and Castle of Abergavenny in his own hands at that time, and though the Castle was not inhabited, the usual officers seem to have been regularly appointed, and from these documents we learn that he was Gentleman Usher to Henry VII, and Constable and Porter of Bergavenny Castle; also, receiver at Bergavenny of the Lord's revenues, and that he also had a grant to farm the demesnes and lands of the Lordship. In the second document he is described as Armiger; but in neither of them is any mention made of Ewyas, nor is it said that he was of any place; the earliest mention of

Ewyas is in Gough's M.S., 1646. Dugdale calls him only Richard Herbert, of Ewyas; but Collins and all other peerages, dub him a Knight. I have not been able to learn any more of the history of this worthy ancestor of so many distinguished families, and I regret much that doubts should be thrown on any part of his reputed history. But in these investigations I am bound to set forth the evidence as I find it, and leave every one to draw his own conclusions.

Before closing the account of the Herbert Monuments it may be as well to mention one other gravestone, inlaid with brass, which is no longer to be found, unless it may be somewhere buried beneath the raised pavement. It is an important tombstone, inasmuch as it gives us valuable genealogical information. We learn of its existence in 1646, from Gough's M.S., in the following words :—" In the same chapel, "between the monuments of Sir William ap Thomas and Sir Richard "Herbert is a fair great flat stone on the ground with this inscrip- "tion. "Underneath this stone lieth buried the body of William "Herbert of Coldbrook, Esq., son and heir of Rees Herbert, Esq., "son and heir of Sir William Herbert, Knight, son and heir of "Sir Richard Herbert, Knight, which William Herbert had three "wives, Denis, Jane, and Anne. By the first he had a son and "a daughter, by the second six sons and five daughters; which "William departed out of this world Anno Dom: 1579." On this "stone is in brass the portraiture of the said William with the "first wife on the right hand, and the portraiture of the two "children under her. And on his left hand his other two wives, and "under the first of them the eleven children had by her. None by "the last there mentioned." In the pedigrees I find no mention of this third wife, nor of the daughter by the first, and of the children by the second, only two sons and three daughters. It is probable that there being no issue, the third wife may have been omitted or forgotten, and it is also likely that the children of the second marriage may have died young or unmarried and so have been unnoticed. The position of the stone is now occupied by the gravestone of Sir James Herbert, of Coldbrook, who died in 1709. It is "a fair great stone" and it is by no means unlikely that at the time of the destructive mutilation of the monuments, not very long after the visit of the writer of the M.S., the brasses may all have been stripped off the stone, which having remained for some 60 years or more without any inscription to indicate whose grave it was, may have been used for the gravestone of Sir James Herbert, and had the present inscription cut upon it. To complete this series it may be of interest to give this inscription on this stone, although it has already been published in Coxe, as it gives much historical information and brings the family down to the year 1709 :—

      HERE LIETH THE BODY OF SIR JAMES
      HERBERT, OF COLDBROOK, KNT.
      WHO DEPARTED THIS LIFE Y^e 6TH

DAY OF JUNE, 1709, IN THE 65th YEAR
OF HIS AGE; HAVING IN HIS
LIFE TIME ENJOYED IN HIS NATIVE
COUNTRY ALL THE CHIEF HONOURS
DUE TO HIS BERTH AND QUALLITY, AS MEMBER
OF PARLIAMENT, &c., AS THEY WERE ENJOYED
BY HIS ANCESTORS EVER SINCE THE REIGN
OF KING HENRY THE FIRST, HE BEING THE
NINETEENTH IN DESCENT FROM HERBERT,
LORD CHAMBERLAIN TO THE SAID KING,
AND NINTH FROM SIR RICHARD HERBERT
OF COLDBROOK, INTERRED UNDER THE TOMB
ON HIS LEFT SIDE, WHO WITH HIS BROTHER
WILLIAM, FIRST EARL OF PEMBROKE OF THAT
NAME, WAS (VALIENTLY FIGHTING *****
KING EDWARD THE FOURTH IN THAT GREAT
GREAT QUARREL BETWEEN THE HOUSES OF YORK
AND LANCASTER) TAKEN PRISONER ****
BANBURY, AND BEHEADED AT NORTHAMPTON
IN THE YEAR, 1469; BOTH THE SAID BROTHERS
BEING SONS OF SIR WILLIAM THOMAS AND
GLADICE DE GAM, WHO ARE INTERRED UNDER
THE MIDDLE TOMB; Ye SAME SIR JAMES
HERBERT LEVEING BEHIND HIM LADY JUDITH
HERBERT, WHO DECEASED THE 12th DAY
OF NOVEMBER THE SAME YEAR. THEY
LEFT BEHIND THEM ONE DAUGHTER, HIS
SOLE HEIR, NAMED JUDITH, MARRIED TO
SIR THOMAS POWELL OF BROADWAY,
IN THE COUNTY OF CARMARTHEN, BARONET,
TO WHOM SHE HATH BORNE SEVERAL SONS
AND DAUGHTERS. HERE ALSO LYETH THE BODY
OF SIR JAMES POWELL, FIFTH SON OF Ye SAID SIR THOS.
POWELL, GRANSON OF Ye SAID SIR JAMES
HERBERT, WHO DIED AN INFANT Ye 11th
DAY OF APRIL, 1709.

No. VII.

EVA DE BRAOSE?

Having completed the series of knightly monuments, we now arrive at the last of the very ancient tombs, namely, those of the two female figures, which although the last, are not the least important either in interest or antiquity, for they are of earlier date than any of the others, and one is of paramount importance. Symonds speaks of these monuments in the following terms : " Between the north yle and quire upon two " altar tombes lyes two statues of women, escocheons on the sides of " this form (giving a sketch of them). One was killed with a fall " following a squirrel from the top of the castle wall. One of the family " of Neville. The other lyes with a peare between her hands, and a " shield very large upon her breast; they say she was choked with a " peare. A Neville, a hound at her feet." These monuments are much earlier than the time of the Nevills, and what was taken for a pear is a heart, by no means an uncommon object to be held between the hands of monumental effigies. The large end of the heart is, however, always turned downwards, which gives the object some resemblance to a pear. They have both been very roughly treated and are sadly injured, especially that represented in photograph IX. which we will now consider. This is the remains of a small raised altar tomb on which there is a recumbent female figure. The head of the tomb now stands close against the pier of the arch between the choir and north aisle, but as the effigy is very much earlier than the present structure of the church which covers it, it may be doubtful whether it is in its original position. But we have only to take it as and where we find it. The effigy is of small size, being only four feet six inches from the feet to so much of the head as now remains, the upper part having been broken away. This rests on two cushions, the lower one square, with a tassel at each corner ; the upper one long, with one tassel at each end. The head is uncovered, the hair being arranged in two long flowing curled ringlets or tresses, on either side of the face, which descend as low as the shoulders, and rest on the tomb below them. The upper part of the head being broken away, we are in ignorance of how the head dress terminated. The figure is represented as wearing a close fitting kirtle or côte hardie, which is closed in the front with a row of close set small flat buttons down to the waist, where it becomes much fuller, and flows down over the feet, the toes only appearing ; these rest on an animal like a dog, but all are very much mutilated. The sleeves fit closely, and seem to terminate in a band above the elbow. There seems to be a close fitting sleeve of an under garment, which descends to the wrist. The right hand lies across the body at the waist, and the left hand held something said by Churchyard to have been a squirrel, and he speaks of it as existing in his time, but it is now broken away. Whatever it was, it seems to have been attached by a chain, which passes over the body with a sweep, and terminates in a slit or pocket in the side of the kirtle, which pocket is of unusual character, being strengthened all round with a very wide margin. The figure is of soft freestone, and both it and the tomb have been sadly broken, and patched up with very rough plaster, so that the details of the costume of the one, and the architecture of the other, are obliterated; but from there being no wimple, and the hair dressed in flowing curls, and from the close fitting gown with tight sleeves, I am disposed to consider it to be of the first half of the XIII. century, and to attribute it to Eva, daughter of William Marshall, Earl of Pembroke, and wife of William de Braose, the last Lord of Abergavenny of that name, who died 1230, leaving only four daughters, all very young. She died 1246, which date will well accord with the costume. The manuscript quoted by Gough states that it was then considered that these two monuments were those of two heiresses of the family of Braose, thus connecting them with this period.

With respect to the history of the squirrel, Churchyard says that the story handed down was that the lady had a pet squirrel which escaped, and she, in trying to recover it, overbalanced herself, and fell from the castle wall, and so lost her life; and that the animal was represented on her tomb in commemoration of the event, and this story is corroborated by what Symonds learned. Such an event is quite possible, and it must be remembered that the ladies of those times were very fond of pet animals, especially small dogs, and as the event was a remarkable one, it is very likely to have been recorded on her tomb. There is no reason to doubt that the squirrel was on the monument; and the peculiarity of the formation of the pocket, with the long chain issuing from it and crossing the body to the hand which held the animal seems to confirm it, as if it had been her practice to carry her pet animal about with her, and on occasions to have placed it in that peculiar pocket, and its escape from there may easily have been the cause of the fatal accident. It may well be doubted if any part of the tomb except the effigy is original.

No. VIII.

EVA DE CANTELUPE.

This is a monument of similar character to the last, but made of a very hard gritstone, containing minute sparkling particles; it has, however, fortunately not suffered quite so much injury. It is also an altar tomb, having the recumbent effigy of a female figure placed upon it. On one side of the tomb are three quatrefoil panels, having within them heater shaped shields, flat on the surface; on the other side in square compartments are six heater shields bowed out on the surface. The two sides of the tomb do not correspond, and the slab itself does not fit the tomb, having only a row of flowers on one side, and rather looks as if it had originally been placed against a wall or in a niche; and the altar tomb has very much the appearance of being a piece of patchwork. The head of it is built so close up against the foot of the last monument, that the present position can hardly be the original; moreover, both the tombs are earlier than the church, it is therefore impossible to conjecture how they have been moved. The mouldings have altogether been destroyed, and there is now nothing to be decyphered on the shields. The figure is, however, remarkably curious and interesting; the total length of it is four feet three inches; the face has unfortunately been much injured. The head rests on an oblong cushion, and is represented as dressed in a wimple, with a veil or couvre chef hanging down behind. The wimple made its appearance as a head tire for women about the end of the XII century, and was a sort of hood, which covered not only the head and shoulders, but was usually brought round the neck beneath the chin, and was occasionally pulled over it, and concealed the whole of the throat. The hair was frequently dressed in plaits or curls, which projected at the sides within the wimple, giving a triangular shape to the head dress, and looking in some instances as if the ears had been unnaturally strained forward. Over this seems to have been worn a sort of close flat topped cap, from which a veil, sometimes called couvre chef or peplum hung down behind, which could be drawn at pleasure over the shoulders and face. The wimple was much worn throughout the XIII century, and in the head dress of nuns is I believe continued to the present day. Along one side of the slab on which the effigy lies, within a hollow, is a row of quatrefoil flowers, alternating with curling leaves of early English character, and the feet rest on a dog. The figure is represented as wearing what appears to be a state mantle, which is gathered up in folds over the arms, the hands being raised upon the breast in prayer, holding between them what seems to be a heart. The most curious and interesting circumstance is that the body of the figure below the hands is covered with a long heater shield, in length twenty-three inches, and in width seventeen across the top, having on it in relief three large fleurs-de-lis, two and one. I am not aware of any similar monument, and I do not think another example exists of a female figure bearing a large knightly shield on her body. This curious peculiarity will, however, enable us to indentify the individual whose tomb and monument it is. The wimple head dress, the border of quatrefoil flowers with the curling leaves, and the heater shield all point to the XIII century, and the coat of arms equally points to the family of Cantelupe, whose arms were gules, three fleurs-de-lis, or; and I have little doubt that I shall be able to indentify it as the monument of Eva de Cantelupe, Baroness of Abergavenny in her own right, which fact will remove all difficulty, and explain every anomaly, for it is an anomaly for a lady to bear on her person the shield of a knight.

It will be remembered that she was daughter and co-heiress of William de Braose, Lord of Abergavenny, which Barony she inherited on the partition of his estates among his four daughters, and conveyed to her husband William de Cantelupe, who thereupon became Lord of Abergavenny, and died in 1256, leaving her, his widow, Baroness in her own right, and as such she was within her own marchership a sovereign Princess, and held the position of one of the barons of the realm, and she had her own tenants by feudal service to follow her standard to the wars, if required; she was therefore a very great and important personage, and this will, I think, quite explain the unusual circumstance of her body in the monument being covered with her shield bearing her coat of arms. She only enjoyed her honours and dignities for a very short time, as she died in 1257, surviving her husband only one year, leaving her son and heir George a minor, whom I have endeavoured to identify as the original of the wooden effigy.

The coat of arms on the shield is of itself of much interest, as it is one of the earliest examples of the arms of Cantelupe, and on so large a scale that there can be no mistake. Archdeacon Coxe was not able to throw any light on the matter, though he mentions the statement in the old manuscript of Gough in 1646, that these female figures were then considered to have been heiresses of the de Braose family, which tends to confirm my identification; but there is also a tendency to mislead by the statement that the three fleurs-de-lis were the arms of the Lords of Werndee. It is quite true that a coat of arms of three fleurs-de-lis are borne as a quartering by families in Monmouthshire, and they are attributed originally to Ynwyr ddu, one of the early reguli or Kings of Gwent in far distant times, before coats of arms were borne and transmitted to families; he was probably a fabulous personage, but this coat was borne by Gwarin ddu, Lord of Gwerndee, and from him find their way among the Herbert quarterings. These arms are per pale az: and sa: three fleurs-de-lis or; but the fleurs-de-lis are generally represented as differently formed, in as much as the leaves issue from or are held together by a narrow oblong band, having sharp pointed corners, and the leaves seem to pass each separately through this band, the centre being the longest, and spreading out in a trifid leaf; whereas in the fleurs-de-lis on the large shield, the upper leaves issue from a large oval plate, three and a half inches long and two inches wide, quite smooth at the edges, and without angle, point, or projection, and in their passage through are united, and issue below in one trefoil leaf. The Cantelupe arms have I believe puzzled many, and among the papers of the late Mr. Wakeman I find the following note respecting them. "The seals " of the Cantelupes present the following different bearings. At first " they appear to have been indifferently gules, three fleurs-de-lis or, and " gules, three leopard's heads or. After a time a fess vair between the " fleurs-de-lis or, leopard's heads, as it may be. Then the two coats com- " bined, gules, three leopard's heads jessant, fleurs-de-lis or; and Lord Can- " telupe at the siege of Carlaverock bore gules, a fess vair, between three " leopard's heads jessant fleurs-de-lis or." And on a seal among his collection of impressions the arms are a fess vair, between three fleurs-de-lis on a heater shield; and the legend on the seal is "S. Willelm de "Cantilupo" in letters of the XIII. or XIV. century—to which William it belonged does not appear. It is to be observed that the name is here spelt Cantilupo, it is however variously written Cantilupe, Cantelupe, and Cantalupe. From this monument it is clear that the arms of the William de Cantelupe who was Lord of Abergavenny were the simple fleurs-de-lis, the leaves issuing from a plain disc. It is well known that a heraldic leopard's head is a lion's front face, the form of it is somewhat round, and the tresses of the mane and beard form projecting points in the circumference, and it is very possible that these oval plates may have been embellished, and changed into leopards by way of difference, or as a mark of cadency by the junior members of the family, still preserving the general character of the bearing. St. Thomas de Cantelupe, the canonized Bishop of Hereford, who was a younger brother of William de Cantelupe, Lord of Abergavenny, bore the arms so changed, and they seem afterwards to have been adopted as the arms of the see. From all these considerations I have no hesitation in coming to the conclusion that this is the tomb and monument of the Lady Eva de Cantelupe, widow of William de Cantelupe and Baroness of Abergavenny in her own right.

No. IX.

JUDGE POWELL.

The next monument is that shewn in photograph XI. and is in the form of an altar tomb, standing in the N.E. corner of the Herbert Chapel, and having two recumbent effigies of a lady and gentleman lying on its top. The body of the tomb is now simply a large block of masonry, coated with plaster, without anything like ornament, except the insertion of two small fragments from some earlier tomb, and one shield of arms, all the ornamental parts having been broken up when the great destruction took place. The figures are very much injured. The costume indicates the latter part of the reign of James I. and beginning that of Charles I. The head of the male figure rests on two cushions, with tassels at the corners. The hair is cut short, and there are moustaches on the upper lip; he wears a ruff round his neck, and is habited in a gown in form resembling that of a master of arts. He wears a doublet, slashed and puffed, as seen by the sleeves as they come through the arm holes of those of the gown. The breeches are also full, and slashed like the doublet, they descend below the knees, and are fastened round the legs with a broad silk sash, tied in a bow at the side, and having the ends fringed. The female has the costume of the same period, but is sadly mutilated and broken.

Archdeacon Coxe informs us that this is the tomb of Sir Andrew Powell and his lady, that they are habited as a monk and nun, that he was an English judge, and Lord Lieutenant of the counties of Hereford, Monmouth, and Brecknock; of course he wrote what was told him, but has fallen into a sad mass of blunders. The costumes at once bespeak the date and the civil condition of the persons, and it is inconceivable how, if ever he looked at the figures, he could have found any resemblance in their dresses to those of a monk and nun, to say nothing of his strange ideas of propriety in the notion of a monk and nun lying side by side. Again, there never was a Sir Andrew Powell among the English judges, but there was a Welsh judge on the Brecon circuit for the counties of Glamorgan, Brecon, and Radnor, named Andrew Powell, from the year 1615 to 1635, just the period indicated by the costume, and he probably is the man, but I do not find him mentioned as a knight, although he may have been one. In 1615 the judges of that Welsh circuit were Sir Walter Pye and Andrew Powell, and in 1635 Sir Walter Pye and Walter Ramsey; it is therefore probable that he died in that year. Lastly, there were then no special Lords Lieutenant for the counties of Monmouth and Brecon. The style of this great officer was at that time " Lord Lieutenant of the Principalities of North and South Wales and the Marches of Wales adjoining thereto;" Brecon being in Wales, and Monmouth in the Marches. These officers or presidents as they were afterwards called, had the power of appointing deputies in the different counties; and being a judge he may very possibly have been so appointed to act in the absence of the Lord Lieutenant or President. The following is a list of the Lords President and Lords Lieutenant of the county of Monmouth, the office of Lord President of Wales and the Marches having been abolished in 1689 :—

LORDS PRESIDENT AND LORDS LIEUTENANT OF THE COUNTY OF MONMOUTH.

1633.—The Earl of Bridgewater was styled in the patent of his appointment of this date "Lord Lieutenant" of the Principalities of North Wales and South Wales, and the Marches of Wales thereto adjoining, and the several counties of Hereford and Salop.—Ob. 1649.

The Commonwealth intervened.

1660.—Richard Vaughan, Earl of Carberry, was appointed Lord President of the Marches on the Restoration, in reward for his services in the Royal cause.

1672.—The Marquess of Worcester, afterwards Duke of Beaufort was appointed Lord President of Wales and Lord Lieutenant of the counties of Gloucester, Hereford, and Monmouth.

1689.—The Duke of Beaufort was succeeded in the Lieutenancy of the county of Monmouth by Charles Earl of Macclesfield, who was also Lieutenant of Breconshire. The office of Lord President was abolished that year.

1694.—7th William III., Thomas, Earl of Pembroke was made Lieutenant of the county of Monmouth, and Thomas Morgan, of Tredegar, Esq., Custos Rotulorum. That office, the chief of the Magistracy, being then separate from the Lord Lieutenancy.

1700.—John Morgan, of Tredegar, was made Custos Rotulorum.

1715.—John Morgan, of Tredegar, was made Lord Lieutenant of the counties of Monmouth and Brecon.—ob. 1720. Being then Custos Rotulorum, he combined the two offices, and since then they have gone together.

1720.—William Morgan, of Tredegar, afterwards Sir William Morgan, K.B., was appointed Lord Lieutenant and Custos of both counties.—Ob. 1731.

1731.—Thomas Morgan, Esq., of Ruperra and Tredegar, was on the death of his brother, Sir William Morgan, appointed Lord Lieutenant and Custos for both counties.—Ob. 1769.

1769.—Thomas Morgan, Esq., of Tredegar, son of the above, made Lord Lieutenant and Custos for both counties.—Ob. 1771.

1771.—Charles Morgan, Esq., of Tredegar, appointed Lord Lieutenant and Custos for both counties.—Ob. 1787.

1787.—The Duke of Beaufort was appointed Lord Lieutenant and Custos of the counties of Monmouth and Brecon.
1803.—The Duke of Beaufort made Lord Lieutenant and Custos of both counties of Monmouth and Brecon.
1835.—Capel Hanbury Leigh, Esq., of Pontypool Park, appointed Lord Lieutenant and Custos Rotulorum of the county of Monmouth.
1861.—Lord Llanover Lord Lieutenant and Custos Rotulorum of the county of Monmouth.
1867.—The Duke of Beaufort Lord Lieutenant and Custos Rotulorum of the county of Monmouth.

It is usually customary to style these high officers Lords Lieutenant; it must, however, be borne in mind that the appointment is the King's or Queen's Lieutenants, and that strictly speaking they are not Lords Lieutenant, unless they are Lords in their own right; but it was generally usual to appoint a Peer, and hence the title.

There is, I think, little doubt that this monument is that of Andrew Powell and his wife; I cannot, however, find of what family of Powell he was a member. There is equally little doubt that his wife was Margaret, daughter of Matthew Herbert, who was great grandson of Sir Richard Herbert of Coldbrook, and is recorded by Mr. Wakeman in a pedigree as having married a Powell; he does not, however, give the Christian name, nor say of what family he came, but simply states that her will is dated 1641. This serves to identify her, for in her will dated 7th January, 1641, she styles herself Margaret Powell, late of Dawkins, in the parish of Bergavenny, and directs that "20s. issuing out of her lands called "y Spittee, should be paid yearly towards the reparacion of the chapel "in St. Mary's Church, Bergavenny, called of the Herbert's Chapel, where "a tomb then prepared for her was situate." From this we may infer that on the death of her husband Andrew in 1635, she prepared a tomb for him and herself in the Herbert Chapel, and I think there is every reason to consider this to be that tomb—for Symonds states that there was "A "faire monument in the same chappel for Judge Powell," and gives a sketch of a coat of arms as on the tomb az. in chief, three castles arg: in base a scaling ladder, impaling Herbert. He has, however, made a mistake in the arms, though the shield bearing the impaled coat which he sketches, may have been destroyed. There was, however, at this time, at the head of the tomb, let in amidst the plaster, an escocheon bearing a single coat, in chief a castle and in base three upright ladders, but no colours are to be perceived, and the whole is so injured and clogged up that no details are to be discovered; the coat, however, is not impaled with Herbert as represented by Symonds, but he may possibly have seen another shield before the destruction of the monument. The correct arms are sa: a spear head imbrued between three scaling ladders arg: on a chief gules, a castle triple towered arg. They were the arms of

Cadivor ap Dinawal, who during one of the frequent feuds between the Welsh and English, is stated to have retaken the Castle of Cardigan by escalade from the Earl of Clare in 1164, and so gained this coat in commemoration of the act, for which he was also rewarded with the Lordship of Castle Howell, and other lands by the Lord Rhys, Prince of South Wales. He was ancestor of the Lloyds of Castle Howell, Maes y Velin or Millfield in Cardiganshire, and Crickadarn in Breconshire, who according to Jones bore these arms. I have not, however, been able to connect them with any family of Powell, though it is very possible that some branch of the family may have adopted the name of Powell as a surname. One of this family, Sir Marmaduke Lloyd of Millfield, was in 1637 appointed chief justice of the great sessions for the several counties of Radnor, Brecon, and Glamorgan, and was therefore a successor to Andrew Powell in that office. His grandson was created a baronet in 1708, but the family became extinct in the male line in 1750.

X.

Dr. DAVID LEWIS.

We now come to the monument of Doctor David Lewis, represented in photograph XII. He was Judge of the High Court of Admiralty in the reign of Queen Elizabeth. This monument, though perhaps not one of very superior artistic execution, is nevertheless one of very great interest, inasmuch as its decorations have all reference to the individual and the office which he held. It is quite unique, and gives information on some matters not to be found elsewhere. He is said to have erected his tomb during his life time, not in those days a very uncommon circumstance, and it seems very probable that he did so, as all the curious details have been very carefully considered, and no ordinary artist would have been likely to know them without his special instruction. This is also an altar tomb, but made of freestone. Its height is three feet four inches to the top of the slab, which is seven feet three inches long, the body of the tomb being six feet six inches in length. It has been said to have been formed out of a single block of stone, but that is clearly not the case, as the body is in two blocks, and the upper slab and base are of course in different pieces. All these details will be seen in the photograph.

The front of the tomb is ornamented with an arcade of three arches, which spring from short broad pilasters, the panels in front of which are filled with three oak leaves or stems; the spandrels between the arches being ornamented with broad leaves, as of water plants on tall stalks, spread out like a fan to fill up the space. In the centre arch is the anchor, the badge and ensign of the admiralty; the ring, cross bar, and flukes have, however, been broken away. The space above the bar of the anchor is filled with oak leaves, which together with those on the pilasters may have reference to the "Hearts of Oak" of which our ships were then built. In the central space below the bar is the following legend in raised capitals, running across the stem of the anchor, JOHN GILDON MADE THIS TO | WME; the W probably belongs to the word TO, though parted from it by the stem of the anchor; if so, neither the grammar nor the spelling are very correct. This, however, may have resulted from the employment of a country sculptor not very well acquainted with the English language, or its orthography. This inscription probably indicates the name of the artist (which name however is not Welsh), otherwise its meaning is not very intelligible, and it is certainly rather a prominent position for the sculptor's name.

In the arch on the left hand are seen three large clasped books, two standing upright, with the third resting upon them, and in the centre, in front of them, is a skull partly broken away. Round these runs a wreath ornamented with scroll work, bearing this legend EN GLORIA MVNDI. This curious device, with the books, skull, and motto must assuredly have had some significance; but no such device or motto is known in the modern court, nor does any one know to what it alludes: it is, however, possible that there might have been found some trace in the old Court of Doctor's Commons before it was dismantled and taken down in 1858. The books in all probability represented certain ancient and important volumes belonging to the court. One may have been the famous "Black Book of the Admiralty," another the laws of Oleron, and the third another ancient volume described by Sir John Exton, who was judge of the court in 1686, as "a thick covered book, with great bosses, kept in the registry, wherein are set some things of antiquity." The Black Book of the Admiralty was described by Exton more than two centuries ago, as containing "ancient statutes of the admiralty, to be "observed both in the ports and havens, upon the high seas and beyond the "seas, engrossed on vellum and written in an ancient hand, in the ancient "French language, which book had been kept in the registry of the court "for the use of the judges." This important book seems to have continued to maintain its place in the archives during the XVIII. century, but it had disappeared before 1808, when enquiries were made for it, and the then officers of the court said they had never seen such a book and knew nothing of it. At what precise period it was written or compiled is not certainly known; Sir John Exton says it is of an ancient hand, not written at once, nor by one person, but the first part in the time of Edward III. or Richard II., and the latter part in the time of Henry IV., V., and VI. Thus its earliest and latest history are enveloped in the clouds of mystery. Some ancient MSS. exist which were probably copies of it. One is in the Cotton Library in the British Museum; one in the Bodleian; and there is also a M.S. copy of it at the Admiralty at Whitehall; and from these Sir Travers Twiss has been enabled to restore and publish "The Black Book of the Admiralty," and its history as far as is known. The laws of Oleron are a code of maritime laws, so called, because they were compiled at the Isle of Oleron, by King Richard I, and were received by all the nations of Europe as the ground of their maritime constitutions. The motto may, therefore, be supposed to apply, either to these precious volumes containing this important and universally approved code of laws or to the court where they were administered; or in the pride of his heart, the judge may have applied the words to the then navy or maritime superiority of England. The meaning of the skull or its reference to the books or motto I am not able to explain.

In the arch on the right hand stands the figure of a man, enclosed within a scroll bearing the legend in raised capitals, THE SARGANT OF THE ADMIRALTEE. This figure therefore represents the sergeant at mace of the High Court of Admiralty in his official dress, which seems to have been a gown with long hanging sleeves. He is represented as a broad shouldered, thickset man, and from the closely trimmed bushy hair, moustache, and beard is very probably a portrait of the actual sergeant at the time. In his left hand he holds a pair of gloves on his breast, and in his right hand he bears the silver oar, as the peculiar mace of the Admiralty Court is termed. This consists of a stem, here represented very short, terminating at the top in a broad blade like that of an oar, on which by careful examination may be discerned on the flat face at the top, a shield with the Royal Arms, France and England quarterly, surmounted by an arched crown, and having as supporters a winged dragon and a greyhound, the supporters of Henry VII, shewing the mace to be of his date ; and below the arms is the Anchor, the badge of the Admiralty. These arms require a practised eye and careful examination with a magnifying glass to distinguish them, but the scaloped wing of the dragon, the dexter supporter, which is the most important point, is clearly to be perceived. I visited the Admiralty Court this spring, and by the kindness of the officers, examined the present mace or silver oar, as it is still called. This form of mace, bearing the same name, is in use at many of the maritime ports where the admiralty jurisdiction extended, and its courts were held at Dover, Yarmouth, Lynn, and some others. Anciently the Admiralty Court used to be held at Doctor's Commons, but since the recent changes it has been accommodated with a temporary court in Westminster Hall. The office of the Sergeant of the admiralty no longer exists, and the officer who is now the mace bearer is termed the Marshal.

The silver oar now in use is not ancient, and differs somewhat in proportion, but not in form from that represented on the monument, being longer in the stem, and shorter in the blade ; but I think it probable that the real proportions may have been somewhat modified in the monument, so as to give a larger surface to the blade for the purpose of better displaying the devices on it ; and I come to that conclusion from what I find on the present mace. The total length is two feet nine inches ; it consists of a stem one foot nine inches long, divided by knops into three parts, from the uppermost of which rises the flat oar blade, one foot in length, spreading out in the shape of that in the monument ; its form therefore is rather that of a paddle. The lower end of the stem terminates in a foot, three inches wide, having the centre of the flat bottom sunk, and in the depression is the anchor and cable rope, round it is engraved "Jasper Swift, Marshial of the Admiralte." There is no date, nor can any record be found to shew when Jasper Swift was marshal ; but as the office was formerly the sergeant, it is probable that Swift may have either been the first marshal after the title of the officer was changed, or when the new mace was made. There are no Hall marks on the blade, but on the stem there are two at the bottom and two at the knop below the blade. The maker's mark consists of the letters I.P. and T.P., being one of each group. There is no annual letter ; one of the other marks is, however, the duty mark, the

Sovereign's head, which is the profile of George III. ; which shews that it must have been made after the year 1784, when the duty on silver plate was first imposed, and the Sovereign's head stamped on all plate made after that time in token of its having been paid ; it must therefore have been made between 1784 and 1820. On the upper part of the blade, at the top, is raised work laid on a shield bearing the Royal arms, France and England quarterly, having for supporters a dragon and a greyhound, the arms and supporters of Henry VII, and surmounted by a high arched crown of the same date, which are exactly the same arms, supporters, and crown as are found on the monument. The middle arch of the crown has been broken away, and in the space thereby rendered vacant has been engraved a modern crown. These arms are of far earlier work than the mace, and have evidently been cut from an earlier mace, and laid on this when it was re-made, but which may very probably have been a copy of the ancient oar. It is very interesting to find the details of the monument thus borne out by the preservation of a portion of the ancient mace in the more recent work. These ancient arms and supporters are but of small size, and would, therefore, not have required so large a blade as that given in the monument. The list of the judges of the High Court of Admiralty is given as far back as 1514, when Christopher Myddleton appears as the first on the list. This date is, however, subsequent to that of the arms on the silver oar. Beneath the Royal arms are those of the Duke of Clarence, afterwards King William IV., who was Lord High Admiral, and the last who held that high office. The arms are surrounded with the garter, and surmounted with his Ducal coronet. This must have been done when he was appointed to that office in 1827, and from the appearance of it, it is very probable that a new blade was then made for the purpose of introducing his arms between the ancient Royal arms and the anchor of the admiralty, which is below them. Both are in relief, and laid on to the flat surface, and the anchor looks as if taken from an earlier mace. The back of the blade is quite plain.

At each end of the tomb is an arch similar to those in the front. In that at the head is an escocheon bearing the arms of Wallis, which were his own family coat, viz : chequy or and sable, on a fess gules three leopard's heads jessant, fleurs-de-lis, or. Within the arch at the foot is a similar escocheon with the coat, p. per pale, a chevron between three oak leaves, slipped ; but to what family these arms belong I am unable to discover, nor do I find any heiress who married into his family who might have borne them.

On the top of the tomb lies the recumbent effigy of the judge, habited in his dress of office ; his head rests on a very small clasped book, beneath which is a very large one, and under this a cushion. There is nothing to indicate what books these were, but their relative sizes suggest a prayer book and bible, if there were any editions published at that time of corresponding sizes. On his head he wears a flat round cap, similar to that worn by Doctors of Civil Law at Oxford, encircled with an ornamental band. Round his neck is a ruff, and he is habited in a doublet, the sleeves of which are buttoned close below the arm down to the wrist and terminate in a ruff. He wears trunk hose and slashed breeches, and his legs are encircled with bands or garters below the knee, having large bows on the outside of the leg. Round his neck are three chains, which lie upon his breast, one below the other, and at his waist hangs a pouch. Over all he wears a short gown, edged with fur, having long hanging sleeves down to the knee, which are full and puckered at the shoulders, and have an opening about the elbow to allow the arm to pass through; the lower part of them seems to be ornamented with spiral or diagonal bands, possibly of broad gold lace. The hands are raised on the breast in prayer, and the toes are broken away, but the feet rest on some object which from the injury it has sustained is not possible to describe, but it very much resembles in shape the hull of a ship of that period; we now proceed to the history of the learned judge himself.

Dr. David Lewis was the eldest son of the Rev. Lewis Wallis, (or Lewis ap John ap Gwilym ap Robert Wallis), vicar of Abergavenny and Llantilio Pertholey, in the time of Henry VIII, by Lucy, daughter of Llewelyn Thomas Lloyd, of Bedwelty, and seems to have taken his father's name Lewis as his permanent surname. He was descended from a junior branch of the family of Wallis of Treowen and Llanarth, the original name being Le Galleys, Le Walleys, Walensis, or Wallis, as written at different periods, the original ancestor being Richard Le Galleys, living in the time of King John. The first of the direct ancestors of Dr. Lewis of whom we have any certain account is a Robert Wallis in the time of Henry VI, but of whom he was the son does not clearly appear. He is called Robyn in the records of Abergavenny, and married Joan, daughter of John Combray, alias Chinn, and had issue Gwilym ap Robert ap Wallis, who married a daughter of Sir William ap Thomas, and had issue John Wallis, who married Margaret, daughter of David Arwydd, and they had issue the Rev. Lewis Wallis, father to Dr. David Lewis; from which time Lewis seems to have been the continued surname of the family. He was born at Abergavenny, and was elected Fellow of All Souls College, Oxford, in the year 1541. He afterwards became Principal of New Inn, and was admitted to the degree of D.C.L. In 1558 he was appointed Judge of the High Court of Admiralty, which post he held to the time of his death. He was named by Queen Elizabeth in the foundation charter of Jesus College, Oxford, the first and original Principal, which post he soon resigned, being at that time a Master in Chancery, and also of the Queen's Court of Requests, as well as Master of St. Catharine's Hospital at the Tower of London. In 1575, he and Sir John Herbert were apppointed joint Commissioners of the

High Court of Admiralty. He was owner of the mansion and manor of Llanthewy Rytherch, which he purchased in 1573 of Philip Jones of London, to whom it had been sold in 1572 by George James, in whose family it had been for some generations. This George James married Joan, the daughter and co-heiress of Sir Charles Herbert of Troy. Dr. Lewis's will is dated 27th March, 1584; he leaves legacies to various relatives mentioned by name, among them is his sister Maud, wife of William Baker, whom he appoints one of his executors, describing him as Recorder of Abergavenny.

Dr. David Lewis died unmarried, 27th April, 1584, and, as we learn from Anthony Wood (Athenœ Oxonienses, Vol. 1, f. 72)" " in the College, " called Doctor's Commons, in London." Of his age nothing is recorded, but if we suppose him to have been twenty-one years of age when elected Fellow of All Souls, 1541, he would have been born in 1520, and so have been sixty-four at the time of his death. " His body was brought down to " be buried in the great church at his native place, and now lies under a " very fair monument, having thereon the ensigns of the admiralty " curiously carved, but without inscription. This monument was built " by him in his life time." Churchyard mentions the monument of his friend Dr. Lewis, then recently deceased, in his account of the church. There can be no doubt that in designing this monument he took considerable care and pains to illustrate correctly many details connected with himself and his office, with a desire to perpetuate and convey to future generations the information which those details contained, and I am well pleased to have been able to illustrate and direct attention to those curious details after the lapse of nearly three centuries.

No. XI.

FIGURE OF JESSE.

We have now arrived at the last of our photographic illustrations, No. XIII. This, however, is not a sepulchral monument, but the remains of a grand example of a Jesse Tree, perhaps the finest and most perfect now to be found. The Tree of Jesse is am emblematical representation of the genealogy of our Saviour from David, formed by a tree growing out of the body of Jesse, the father of David, who lies asleep, on the branches of which are represented by small statues among the foliage, or in the case of a window by paintings on the glass of the different personages through whom he is descended. The idea seems to have been suggested by the eleventh chapter of Isaiah, in the first and following verses. This figure is the colossal statue of a man representing Jesse, lying asleep, and reclining on his right side. The head, which has a long flowing beard, is covered with a cap, and reposes on a cushion supported by an angel; the body and legs being clothed with folds of drapery. From the left side of the body issues the stem of the tree, which is usually a vine, and is grasped or supported by the left hand of the figure, above which it is cut short off. These Jesse Trees are by no means common, and are more usually represented in windows; but they were occasionally made to form the reredos of an altar. Such an altar existed formerly in the fine church of St. Cuthberts at Wells, but was mutilated and destroyed at the reformation, the remains of it having since been discovered. There is also a very fine example in the Priory Church at Christchurch, Hants, where the reredos represents the Stem of Jesse, who lies asleep above the altar, whilst a vine stem proceeds upwards from his body, and ramifies into the various niches, each of which has its statue. There is a fine Jesse window in the chapel of the college at Winchester, but of modern glass copied from the old; and there is also a very celebrated one in the east window of Dorchester Church, Oxfordshire, where some of the figures are sculptured and form part of the mullions, others being painted on the glass. The east window of St. Georges, Hanover Square, is also a Jesse window, which seems to be Swiss glass of about the date 1500, the original glass having been divided to fit it into the Palladian structure. There are also some instances known on the continent.

The only full description of a Jesse Tree that I can find is in the Iconographie Chretienne, where such a tree is figured in a wood cut, with the following description: "We should leave incomplete the "Iconographic history of the Virgin Mary, if we did not speak here of "the Tree of Jesse, which is met with so often at the close of the XII. "century. Jesse asleep serves in some sort as the root of the mysterious "Stem, which issues sometimes from his breast, sometimes from his "mouth, and sometimes from his brain. Branches diverge from this "stem, and bear on their extremities one of the ancestors of our Saviour; "at the summit one full blown flower serves as the throne of Mary, "sometimes alone, at other times holding in her arms the divine Child." It is therefore such a subject as we might well expect to find forming part of an altar in a church dedicated to the Virgin. In the engraving the figure of Jesse is represented exactly as we find him here, viz:—a man asleep reclining on his right side, clad in a flowing robe, and wearing a cap on his head, which rests on a cushion; this, however, is not supported by an angel. From the body issues the tree, which consists of an upright stem, having on either side three branches diverging from it, on each of which are represented two or three statues of Kings or other personages, twelve in all; whilst the central stem terminates in a full blown flower which supports the standing figure of the Virgin, bearing the Child in her arms, and surrounded with an oval Glory.

This wooden figure is mentioned by Churchyard in the marginal notes to his poem, "In this church was a most famous worke in manner of a "genealogy of Kings, called the Roote of Jesse, which worke is defaced, "and pulled down in pieces." It is also mentioned by Symonds in 1645, who says "At the east end of the north yle church lyes a large "statue for Jesse, and a branch did spring from him, and on the boughs "divers statues, but spoyld." It must then have been lying under the window in the Lewis Chapel. It was most likely that it was pulled down at the time of the Reformation, and there does not seem now to remain a vestige of it except the grand figure of Jesse, the root of the tree, which is in good preservation, and a remarkably fine example of bold oak carving of the XV. century, if not of earlier date. Its size and weight are unusually large, its length being ten feet. It must have been a grand and "famous worke" as Churchyard calls it, and have occupied a very conspicuous and important position in the church; and if it is allowable to hazard a conjecture, without however any authority, I should be disposed to think it originally formed the reredos of the High Altar, and so have formed part of the screen between the choir and the Lady Chapel, which I have ventured to consider as having occupied what is now the present chancel. Wherever it stood, it must have been a magnificent object, and a grand specimen of carving in oak; and it is not unlikely that it was embellished with painting and gilding. The fragments of it remained at the time of Churchyard's visit in 1586, and from his expression it seems to have been much renowned at that time, though more than thirty years after its destruction. At the bottom of the beard, where the curls part, is a small cavity, but whether it ever contained a relic, or was designed to contain one is uncertain; there is no appearance of any rebate to receive a glass.

The figure was placed in its present position at the time of the great alterations in 1828, and now reposes on a bed, the front of which seems to have been constructed with portions of the sides of some altar tomb, and consists of eight shallow niches or panels, the upper parts of which terminate in cinquefoiled ogees, and are capped with crocketed ogee canopies, springing from small pinnacled buttresses, which divide the panels, in each of which stands a small statuette. The work is in freestone, and has been much injured; it seems to be of the latter part of the XIV. century, and may very possibly have been a portion of the tomb of Lord Hastings, whose date it will suit, which was removed from the middle of the church by "fine device of man," and worked up into a porch, and when the porch was at some subsequent time removed, the panelling may very well have been used to form a bed for the support of the Root of Jesse.

This closes the series of monuments of which photographs have been taken. The ancient monuments, however, in the Priory Church are by no means exhausted, for there still remain both monuments, slabs, brass plates, and memorial inscriptions, which though not of equal importance with those which have come under our consideration, are still of interest, and deserving of consideration and attention.

www.ingramcontent.com/pod-product-compliance
Lightning Source LLC
Chambersburg PA
CBHW020300090426
42735CB00009B/1164